GCSE HOSPITALITY and CATERING

THE ESSENTIALS

Judy Gardiner

Jacqui Housley

HODDER
EDUCATION
PART OF HACHETTE LIVRE UK

Every effort has been made to trace and acknowledge ownership of copyright. The publishers will be glad to make suitable arrangements with any copyright holders whom it has not been possible to contact. The authors and publisher would like to thank the following for permission to reproduce copyright illustrative material:

Adam Woolfitt/Corbis, p15t; Anthony Blake/photolibrary.com, p19; Barking Dog Art, pp22, 23, 24m, 49b; Carl Drury, pp56t, 57b, 59b; David Mack/Science Photo Library, p44t; David Scharf/Science Photo Library, p43b; Dominic Dibbs/photolibrary.com, p41; Electronic Temperature Instruments Ltd, p46b; Eye of Science/Science Photo Library, p44 2nd, 3rd from top, 44b; F. Fink Jr Benjamin/photolibrary.com, p87t; ImageState/Alamy, p92b; Ingram Publishing, pp30m, 33, 37t, 38, 65b, 66b, 67t, 69, 70t, 76, 81, 98, 99, 105t, 110t/b, 112, 128t, 134, 136, 138, 140, 141, 143, 145; Jeff Greenberg/Alamy, pp16b, 63; Justin Kase/Alamy, p100; Lightworks Media/Alamy, p111b; Olaf Doering/Alamy, p108t; Pablo Paul/Alamy, pp46m, 131t; Photodisc, pp1m, 5t, 13b, 16t, 58b, 103, 104t, 113; Profimedia International s.r.o./Alamy, p12; Rob Wilkinson/Alamy, p117; Sam Bailey, pp27, 28m, 30t, 31, 34t, 35, 36, 42, 45b, 60t, 62b, 66t, 108m; Scimat/Science Photo Library, pp43m, 44 2nd from bottom; Scott Rothstein/istockphoto.com, p62t; Tom Hussey/The Image Bank/Getty Images, p18b; Visit Wales, p115m.

Via Fotolia.com, ©: Adam Kulesza, p115b; Ade Hughes, p74b; Alfonso d'Agostino, p13t; Alison Bowden, p132; Andrea Seemann, p122b; Andrejs Pidjass, p45m; Bartosz Ostrowski, p84; Chantal Seigneurgens, p5m; Christine Nichols, p28t; Dmitry Goygel-Sokol, p10; Douglas Dean, p17; Edyta Pawlowska, p64; Elena Kalistratova, p58t; Elke Dennis, p75; Eric Lecas, p59t; Erwin Layaoen, p70b; Francesco Ridolfi, p61t; Francois E. du Plessis, p7; Jacob Wackerhausen, p125; Jean-Louis Vosgien, p82b; John Panella, pp28b, 118b; Jostein Hauge, p87b; Kirill Livshitskiy, p86m; Leah-Anne Thompson, p57t; Leonid Nyshko, p45t; Linda Hewell, pp34, 110m; Lisa Eastman, p82t; Lori Sparkia, p80; Marti Timple, p8; Matthew Hayward, p70m; Maxim Efimov, p119t; Michael Chamberlin, p1b; Michelangelo Gratton, p3b; Monika Adamczyk, p29; Nataliya Kuznetsova, p79; Nicola di Nozzi, p124; Nicola Gavin, p1t; Nikolay Suslov, p3t; Norman Pogson, p107; Paco Ayala, p18t; Paul M, p72; Pavel Losevsky, p105b; Peter Spiro, pp106, 122t; Petr Vaclavek, p65t; Richard Johnson, p61b; Robert Byron, p67; Roman Milert, pp4, 118t; Roman Mostakov, p123; Roy Shakespeare, p2; Selcuk Arslan, p122m; Simone van den Berg, p56; Stef Feijen, p119b; Stephen Finn, p92t; Stephen McWilliam, p15b; Suhendri Utet, p47b; Susanne Güttler, p37b; Sylvie Peruzzi, p108b; Tomasz Stelmach, p127; Troy McCullough, p88; Uyen Le, p24t; Wai Heng Chow, p131b; Yekaterina Choupova, p30b.

The Good Food Guide 2008 cover image (115t) reproduced with kind permission of Which?
t = top, m = middle, b = bottom of page

This material has been endorsed by WJEC and offers high quality support for the delivery of WJEC qualifications. While this material has been through a WJEC quality assurance process, all responsibility for the content remains with the publisher.

Orders: please contact Bookpoint Ltd, 130 Milton Park, Abingdon, Oxon OX14 4SB. Telephone: (44) 01235 827720. Fax: (44) 01235 400454. Lines are open from 9.00–5.00, Monday to Saturday, with a 24 hour message answering service. You can also order through our website www.hoddereducation.co.uk.

British Library Cataloguing in Publication Data
A catalogue record for this title is available from the British Library

ISBN: 978 0 340 94839 2

First Published 2007
Impression number   10 9 8 7 6 5 4 3
Year   2012 2011 2010 2009 2008

Copyright © 2007 Judy Gardiner and Jacqui Housley

Cover photo © ErickN – FOTOLIA.
Typeset by Pantek Arts Ltd, Maidstone, Kent.
Illustrations by Oxford Designers and Illustrators.
Printed in Italy for Hodder Education, a part of Hachette Livre UK, 338 Euston Road, London NW1 3BH.

Contents

CONTENTS

Introduction

This book has been written to fill a need for a basic theory book to support students studying GCSE Catering and GCSE Hospitality and Catering. However, it is also aimed at other school or college students who are interested in, or studying, catering and other hospitality courses. The book is not intended as a definitive text book that contains all the answers, but as a student-friendly guide that contains the essentials presented in a fun and accessible way.

The book has been designed so that topics are easily found. Much of the information is presented in chart or list form to minimise the amount of written text. It has been written to help students to complete coursework successfully and to provide them with information for independent study and revision. Activities are provided to help students check and improve their knowledge and understanding. Key words have been highlighted for quick and easy reference. There are sample GCSE questions at the end of the book to help students develop their examination technique.

It is hoped that students and teachers will find the contents interesting, useful and easy to follow.

Dedication

The authors would like to thank their respective families for their unfailing support while writing the book, and other teachers for their encouragement and positive comments.

The authors and publishers would like to thank Jean Batchelor, Allison Candy, Mary Stevens and Kay Walters for their advice and guidance in the development of this book. We would particularly like to extend our gratitude to Brigid O'Regan of WJEC, whose contribution has been invaluable from concept to publication.

Specification mapping grid

The book has been designed to follow the Hospitality and Catering GCSE specification most closely.

- Students studying for the Hospitality and Catering Single Award will need to study Unit 1 and either Unit 2 or 3.
- Students studying for the Hospitality and Catering Dual Award will need to study all four units.
- Students studying GCSE Catering will need to follow Units 1, 3 and 4 and the practical assessment guidelines in Unit 2.

INTRODUCTION

UNIT I

WHAT IS THE HOSPITALITY AND CATERING INDUSTRY?

The hospitality and catering industry is very diverse. A hospitality and catering establishment is defined as one that provides food, drink and/or accommodation. This is known as a product-and-service provider.

Many different kinds of commercial (for money) businesses operate in the hospitality and catering industry, but there are also non-commercial businesses in the industry.

Types of establishment

Residential accommodations include:

- hotels
- guest houses
- holiday parks
- farmhouses that offer accommodation
- public houses that offer accommodation
- bed-and-breakfast establishments.

Non-residential establishments only provide food. These include:

- restaurants
- cafes
- fast-food outlets
- public houses
- wine bars
- delicatessen and salad bars
- take-away outlets
- school meals and transport catering
- burger vans.

There are also non-commercial residential establishments within the industry. These include:

- hospitals
- residential homes
- prisons
- armed services.

Contract caterers

There are also caterers who provide food and drink for a function where catering facilities are not already provided. These are known as contract caterers.

They prepare the food for functions such as, weddings, banquets, garden parties and parties in private houses. They may prepare and cook the food in advance and deliver it to the venue, or they may cook it on site. They may also provide staff to serve the food, if required. Contract caterers are used by a wide range of organisations as it relieves them of the pressures involved in catering for such events.

Types of service and client groups

There is a range of client groups who require different services from the industry.

Businesses

These often use facilities and services in relation to work, such as conference facilities, food and accommodation for meetings, training sessions and other courses. These services are usually paid for by the business. They may use contract caterers to provide food and drinks for in-house meetings.

Private

This is where a customer's individual demands are met. Private events may include weddings and parties and can be held in a variety of establishments, such as hotels, restaurants, local venues or at home.

Groups

This section includes tourists, associations, clubs etc. They have a variety of catering requirements. For example, the 'Young Farmers' group may want outdoor catering, such as a barbeque. Some customers have special requirements because of their culture or dietary needs. Customers can also be grouped into ages i.e. children, young people, adults, elderly people. Each group will have their own needs.

ACTIVITY
Find out about the different types of catering establishments in your area and match them with the type of client group they provide for. How many can you find?

Job descriptions

There is a range of jobs available in the hospitality and catering industry.

They can be split into five main groups:

- management and administration
- food preparation
- front-of-house
- food and drink service
- accommodation.

Within each of these groups there are various jobs. Let's look briefly at each area.

Management

There may be a manager for all the different areas of a large establishment, but only one in a smaller place. Within a larger company there may be:

- a manager, who is in charge of the day-to-day running of the company, and is responsible for making a profit and organising every area.
- an assistant manager, who is responsible to the manager and may have work delegated to him by the manager. He/she will also be in charge in the manager's absence.

Chefs

Depending on the size of the establishment, there may only be one chef with a kitchen porter to help, or there may be a whole brigade of chefs. A 'brigade' is the term used for a group of chefs in a kitchen. There are several different kinds:

- The head chef is the person in charge of the kitchen. In a large establishment, this person has the title of 'executive chef'. The executive chef is a manager who is responsible for all aspects of food production, including menu planning, purchasing, costing, planning work schedules, and hygiene.
- The second (sous) chef ('soo shef') is directly in charge of production. Because the executive chef's responsibilities require spending a great deal of time in the office, the sous chef takes command of the actual production and the minute-by-minute supervision of the staff. Both the

sous chef and executive chef have had many years of experience in all stations of the kitchen.

- The pastry chef (patissier) ('pa-tees-syay') prepares pastries and desserts.
- The larder chef (garde manger) ('gard-mawn-zhay') is responsible for cold foods, including salads and dressings, patés, cold hors d'oeuvres, and buffet items.
- The sauce chef (saucier):('so-see-ay') prepares sauces, stews, and hot hors d'oeuvres, and sautés foods to order. This is usually the highest position of all the stations.
- The vegetable chef (entremetier): (awn-truh-met-i-ay) prepares vegetables, soups, starches, and eggs. Large kitchens may divide these duties among the vegetable cook, the fry cook, and the soup cook.
- The assistant chef (commis) helps in all areas of the kitchen, generally doing the easier tasks. The commis may be completing basic training to become a chef.
- The kitchen porters clean up after the chefs, do the washing and carry goods to and from the store.

Front-of-house

Again, depending on the size of the establishment, this role may be taken on by the owner, or staff will be employed to do it. Front-of-house roles include:

- the head receptionist, who is responsible for taking the bookings and ensuring the staff are given the correct information. The receptionist is the first person the customer comes into contact with. They help customers check in, and deal with any complaints. They inform other departments about room bookings, and may also complete staff rotas and deliver staff training.
- the assistant receptionist, who assists the head receptionist, helps customers to check in, deals with bills and answers the phone.
- the porter, who delivers cases to rooms and helps in setting up rooms for conferences etc.
- the night porter, who covers the reception at night and ensures any complaints or queries are dealt with effectively.

Food and drink service

This section covers the staff who serve food and drink to the customers. These staff are collectively known as 'wait staff'. They may include:

- the restaurant manager, who is in charge of the restaurant. The manager takes bookings, relays information to the head chef, arranges training for staff, completes rotas and ensures the restaurant runs smoothly.
- the head waiter/ess, who is second in charge of the restaurant. They greet and seat customers and relay information to the staff. They may also deal with complaints.
- the wine waiter/ess, who is responsible for helping guests to select wine. They serve the wine and other alcoholic drinks to customers.
- the wait staff, who serve the customers, clear the tables and check that the customers are satisfied with the service.

Accommodation operations

These are the staff who look after the rooms that are available to hire. These roles could include:

- conference manager - responsible for organising conferences for groups and making sure the group's needs are met on the day
- head housekeeper - responsible for seeing that all the rooms are ready for customers, completing rotas for staff, telling staff what rooms need to be cleaned, checking laundry.
- housekeeper - responsible for allocating jobs to chambermaids, checking laundry and toiletries, checking rooms are cleaned correctly.
- chambermaid - cleans the rooms, changes the beds, checks that there are enough toiletries, clean towels etc.
- maintenance officer - completes any repairs that can be done in-house, and gets in specialist maintenance staff (e.g. gas) when required.

Most people who go into the hospitality and catering industry are able to work their way up to the position they would like. Larger establishments offer the opportunity to work in a range of areas and provide training on the job. The advantage of this is that you can earn at the same time as you are training. You can also go on day-release, or attend college full time. It is a great industry to be involved in and you can often meet famous people.

KEY WORDS:

Management: the people who are in charge of specific areas.
Chefs: the staff who are responsible for preparing and cooking the food.
Front-of-house: the reception area of the establishment.
Food and drink service: the serving area in a restaurant, café, bar.
Accommodation services: the housekeeping side of an establishment.

ACTIVITY

Find out what jobs are available in your area. Research how you can progress up the ladder and what qualifications you would need to be able to do the job.

With the help of your teacher, carry out a mock interview for a job you would like to do.

List the personal skills you would need to work in the hospitality and catering industry.

COMMUNICATION AND RECORD-KEEPING

What types of communication and record-keeping are necessary in the hospitality and catering industry?

Let's look at the types of communication used and what they are used for.

Types of communication	Use
Verbal	Giving instructions to others, talking to clients, taking messages.
Written	Confirmation of bookings, memos, promotions, letters, taking orders for food and drink.
Telephone	Taking messages, giving responses.
Fax	Information, ordering, newsletters, internal memos.
ICT	Staff rotas, bookings, accounts, invoices, room management, booking events and functions, orders, stock control.

It is important that record-keeping is accurate and appropriate. This enables staff to check on a booking or an order, without the need for the member of staff who took the booking or placed the order to be there.

Communication is important across all areas of the industry. Each department has to know what is happening. For example, if the reception did not tell the chef or head waiter how many people had booked in, they would not know how many to cater for or to set covers for. Or if the chef did not tell the wait staff what foods were available, the wait staff could not tell the customers, who may then order something that is not on the menu.

Staff have to communicate effectively with each other to ensure things get done quickly. They also have to communicate well with customers. It is important that customers feel they can approach the staff if they require assistance or if there is a problem.

To communicate well, staff should:

- be friendly
- be smart
- be clean
- have good verbal communication skills
- have good written skills
- be able to use ICT effectively.

In the hospitality and catering industry, it is usual to work as a member of a team. This might be in the kitchen (as one of the kitchen brigade), in the restaurant (as one of the restaurant brigade), in the accommodation operations or front-of-house. Sometimes teams are called groups. Every member of staff needs to feel part of a group or team. The hospitality and catering industry relies heavily on 'teamwork' to provide the products and services the customer wants.

How do teams work?

In an organised team such as the kitchen brigade, every member of the team has a responsibility in the production of food. Each kitchen brigade will have a definite structure and set procedures. The team leader (i.e. the head chef) will:

● decide who works in the team
● decide what the team has to do
● take responsibility for the standard of work produced
● make sure that current legislation standards are met.

Stages in teamwork

Teams go through several stages before they are able to achieve excellent standards.

Stage 1

The team is given a task. Each person in the team has to understand what the task is and the best way of achieving a good end result.

Example: Your team/group has been asked to plan a menu for the retirement party for your head teacher. What other information will you need before deciding on the menu?

Stage 2

The team goes through a stage of 'disagreement' when different ideas are put forward and discussed.

Example: Your team/group cannot decide whether to have a buffet or a sit-down meal for the party.

Stage 3

The team starts to work together as one unit, instead of one person trying to dominate the others or get all their ideas chosen.

Example: Your team/group decides to accept a majority decision and then everyone works together to plan the best menu.

Stage 4

The team works very well together.

Example: Your team/group plans a buffet menu that will suit all dietary needs.

How can you recognise good teamwork?

- Team members communicate (talk to each other) effectively.
- Team members feel able to suggest ideas.
- Team members know what is expected of them.
- Team members 'share' responsibility to make sure that tasks are done.
- Tasks are carried out quickly.
- Tasks are carried out effectively.
- Team members are happy in their jobs.
- Team members have high self-esteem.

What affects team behaviour?

- Strong personalities that want to dominate.
- Individual characteristics i.e. qualities of team members.
- Cultural differences.
- Social skills of team members.
- Conflicts or personality clashes within the team.
- Pressure.
- Stress.
- Change i.e. in home circumstances or working practices.
- Attitude and behaviour of the team leader.

How can you recognise good team leaders?

Team leaders or supervisors often have very good technical skills, knowledge and ability. Good team leaders should be able to:

- delegate tasks effectively
- motivate their teams
- communicate effectively
- give advice, support and training
- help team members to develop performance
- maintain quality
- monitor the work of team members
- give praise
- recognise individual contribution to the team
- give constructive and positive feedback
- check the team is meeting its objectives – whether it is meeting financial targets or gaining a Michelin star!

Problem-solving

Problems occur in the hospitality and catering industry all the time. Often there are *immediate* solutions to a problem but some problems need a more *long-term* solution.

Here are two examples:

1. The soup is cold.
   Immediate response: apologise, take back to kitchen, replace or offer alternative.
   Long-term response: refer to head chef to make sure correct training and checking procedures are in place.
2. A tap is dripping in a hotel bedroom.
   Immediate response: Send maintenance to fix problem. This will prevent accidents, water damage and loss of water.
   Long-term response: Regular checking, reporting, maintenance and repair.

Dealing with problems and complaints becomes easier with practice but there are 'set' procedures to follow. It is useful to practise these procedures in a 'safe' environment, such as a school restaurant, or by doing role-plays within your group. This will help to build your confidence.

Every establishment will have its own rules and regulations. What you are allowed to do will depend upon your position or level of responsibility. For example, you would not be allowed to offer a discount or vouchers to a customer who complains if you had just started a job as a waiter in a local restaurant – you would need to ask your supervisor to deal with the situation.

Typical complaints procedure

If a customer complains about the food or service in the restaurant you should:

- Stay calm. Listen attentively to what the customer has to say (some customers find it difficult to complain, so once they start they do not want to be interrupted!).
- Apologise.
- Try to resolve the situation. For example, if the food is cold or not up to standard in some other way, take it back to the kitchen and report it to the head chef and the restaurant manager. Offer the customer a replacement or an alternative dish.
- Explain to the customer what you intend to do (e.g. bring their replacement dish within five minutes, if they have agreed that this is acceptable, or ask the restaurant manager to deal with their concerns).
- Apologise again for the problem.

Handling compliments

Sometimes you will receive compliments, especially if you give good service or if customers enjoy the meal you serve. Some staff find this just as difficult to deal with as complaints.

When you receive a compliment you should do the following:

- Thank the customer for their comments and show you are pleased to receive the compliment.
- Ask if you could do anything to improve next time!
- Pass on compliments to others, especially to the chefs if the compliments are about the food.

REMEMBER

Remember that you may not have the authority to offer free drinks, money off the bill or vouchers, so seek the help of someone who has.

Why do we need customer care?

- Most hospitality and catering establishments rely on income from customers.
- Customers will be satisfied if their needs are met.
- Customers who are satisfied will come back.

To achieve good customer care you need to:

- put your customers first
- make them feel valued and important
- make them feel comfortable and safe
- make them want to return.

How customers enjoy their 'meal experience', whether in a fast-food outlet or high-class restaurant, depends on:

- the welcome or greeting they receive when they first arrive
- the décor - bright and colourful or warm with dim lights
- the atmosphere - lively or quiet
- the hygiene – the outlet needs to be clean and well presented (especially the toilets)
- the safety – fire exits need to be clearly marked
- the security – customers' belongings need to be safe
- the way customers' behave – if they are too noisy it may affect the enjoyment of others
- where the table is situated – quiet corner or centre of dining area
- the presentation of the menu and drinks list
- whether all menu items are available
- the speed, efficiency and quality of service
- polite and helpful staff
- attentive staff
- the quality of the food
- value for money
- how questions are answered
- how problems and complaints are handled
- how the bill is presented and payment taken
- how customers' are treated when they leave.

Good customer care in a restaurant means staff doing their best to make sure customers enjoy their 'meal experience.'

What are standards of customer care?

Imagine you are a customer visiting a restaurant for the first time. What are you looking for? What are you expecting?

Your answers are the 'standards' of customer care you expect.

They may include:

- a clean and well presented entrance
- a warm welcome from head waiter, restaurant manager or receptionist
- sample menu and drinks list are on display
- staff who are smartly dressed and well groomed
- staff who smile when they speak to customers
- customers are shown to their tables quickly
- if there is a delay, staff apologise and give a reason
- customers are served efficiently
- staff who are polite and attentive
- staff who are helpful
- staff who understand customers' needs
- staff who have a professional attitude
- staff who make each customer feel special
- staff who escort customers to the door at the end of the meal and say 'Have a good day' or 'Goodnight'.

Look at the picture below and say what you would need to do as restaurant manager to sort out the problems and keep customers happy.

A range of food service systems are available. These include:

- counter service – cafeteria service, multi-point, free-flow, fast-food, vended service, seated counter service, buffet and carvery
- table service – waiter or waitress service
- transported meal systems – e.g. meals on aeroplanes
- cooking and/or service of food from a trolley in front of customers – e.g. Gueridon service.

Sometimes, more than one type of service operates within the same establishment. A central production area may send food to a variety of different outlets within one area.

Types of counter service

Cafeteria service

This is the most versatile of all food service systems. A menu is displayed at the entrance to the cafeteria.

- Customers 'flow' past a display of food and select the items they want. Some of the meal items (usually hot items such as main courses) may be served by staff from behind the counter.
- Payment is made before the customer eats. It is easy for staff to display the menu and stock the displays.
- Cutlery and condiments are placed after the tills to keep a steady flow.
- The dining area is regularly cleaned.
- Some areas of the dining room may be kept for customers eating meals rather than snacks at busy times.

Free-flow

This is similar to the cafeteria system, except that customers go straight to the food or drink counter they want. It avoids unnecessary queuing but is not good for people who want a full range of items.

Multi-point

This is like the free-flow system, but has separate trays, tills, cutlery and condiment areas. It's not good for customers who want a full range of items.

Fast-food

In fast-food outlets, the customer orders and collects the meal from one of a number of service points along the service counter.

- At each service point there is a cash till and a member of staff who takes the order, receives the payment, collects the food and drinks ordered and assembles them on a tray, to be eaten in the restaurant or in a bag or container to be taken away.
- The food is usually shown in photographs above the counter. The complex tills record all the orders, time, method of payment etc. and give a complete breakdown of sales and other information to head office. Speed is essential.
- Fast-food outlets are very expensive to set up and need expensive equipment (fryers, griddles etc.). A fast-food outlet will not survive unless it has a high turnover of customers.

Many take-away restaurants, such as fish and chip shops and Chinese take-aways, use a similar method but only have one service point behind the counter.

> **ACTIVITY**
> Find out about the types of service offered in food outlets in your area. How many different ones can you find?

Vended service

This is used widely in large buildings, such as hospitals, hotels and factories, where food and drink are needed throughout the day and night.

- Vending machines 'sell' a wide range of products such as sweets, drinks, packaged snacks and even whole plated meals.
- Some are 'coin operated' some are operated by special discs or cards issued to staff, some are 'free vend' i.e. operated by the touch of a button.

- Vending machines offer ideal portion control and good hygiene standards (food is always packaged).
- They need careful maintenance and regular stocking.
- High turnover is important. Vending machines are often placed next to microwaves so that customers can buy 'chilled' food and re-heat before eating i.e. Buy – Reheat – Serve – Eat.

Seated counter service

Customers are seated at the counter, usually on stools, and are served by staff behind the counter. Often used in situations where customers are on their own (e.g. railway stations and airport terminals).

Buffet service

Customers select their meal items from an open counter or buffet table. The customers help themselves to everything, or the serving staff serve some or all of the items. Serving staff often serve the meat items as these are the most expensive, leaving customers to help themselves to salads etc.

Carvery service

In this case, starters, drinks and sweets are served by the serving staff.

- Customers collect their own main course items from the carving table where the joints of meat are displayed and kept hot by special lamps and hot plates.
- Often, a chef from the kitchen carves the joints, but sometimes a member of the serving staff does the carving.
- Customers help themselves to vegetables, gravy, sauces and other accompaniments like Yorkshire puddings.
- Carveries are particularly popular for Sunday lunch.

Table service

Waiter/waitress service

This is used when a more personal service is needed.

- It is more expensive than a counter service, because of the number of staff involved.

- For large functions (e.g. wedding receptions and banquets) a waiter/waitress can serve many more people than in the usual restaurant service.
- When tables are laid up banquet style, one waiter/waitress would serve the people on both sides of an 'aisle' i.e. serve the left-hand side of one table and the right-hand side of the other table.

Transported meal systems

The most well known type of transported meals is airline food. This is used most commonly on long-haul flights, where passengers choose hot food from a limited menu.

How the airline food system works:

1. Airline representatives choose from a selection of prepared foods.
2. Food is prepared in the kitchens away from the airport.
3. Meals for special diets are ordered and prepared in the correct quantities by the kitchen.
4. Meals are plated, covered and blast chilled.
5. Meals are placed on trolleys covered with dry ice pellets to keep the food fresh.
6. The trolleys are delivered to the correct flights and stored in the kitchen area of the plane.
7. Before service the meals are re-heated and placed in heated trolleys.
8. Passengers then get a limited choice of meals on the plane.

Advantages:

- Children and special diets are catered for.
- The airline orders the right amount of dishes so there is less waste.
- First- and business-class passengers can pre-order their meals in advance.

Disadvantages:

- There are no 'second helpings'.
- The choice is limited to two dishes.
- Passengers do not always like the choices available.

The Gueridon system

This style of service is used with à la carte or table d'hôte menus. The food is carved or 'finished' at a table or trolley placed next to the customer's table. A spirit lamp is used to finish cooking portions of poultry, meat or fish. Some dishes are completed in this way, with a flambé technique or sauce. Two popular dishes are Steak Diane and Crèpes Suzette. This form of service requires highly skilled staff who can cook and present the food attractively and can work confidently with a little bit of 'showmanship'.

Nutrition links to healthy eating and menu planning.

Healthy eating is important at any age. Along with regular exercise, avoiding excess alcohol and stress and not smoking, a healthy diet can contribute to a healthy life-style.

Good nutrition is very important. It is needed for 'normal' growth and development. Once we mature we need to continue to eat well in order to maintain good health and fight off infections.

It is very rare to hear of starvation (severe lack of food) in the UK. However, there are serious health concerns about malnutrition (poor nutrition i.e. eating the wrong type of food) which leads to dietary-related diseases such as obesity, anorexia, Type 2 diabetes, osteoporosis (brittle bone disease) and heart disease.

Nutrients

These are the chemicals found in food. The main nutrients are:

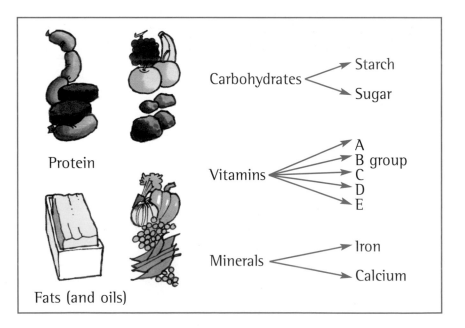

Water and fibre are also very important to include in the diet, but they are not classed as nutrients.

It is important to know which nutrients are in particular foods so that we can maintain a healthy diet.

What is a healthy balanced diet?

You may have heard of a 'balanced diet' but wondered what it really means. It does not mean eating the same amount of each food every day! It means eating a variety of foods each day, including foods from each of the four main food groups shown below.

Eating the recommended portions of the following food groups each day will help to make sure you get a balanced range of nutrients including the vitamins and minerals your body needs.

Meat and meat alternatives (e.g. fish, quorn, soya products)	2 portions
Milk and other dairy products	3 portions
Fruit and vegetables	5 portions
Potatoes and other starchy foods (e.g. rice, pasta, bread, cereals)	5–6 portions

A balanced diet

Try to eat wholegrain products when possible e.g. wholemeal bread (instead of white bread), whole wheat cereals like Weetabix and Shredded Wheat (instead of sugar-coated cereals), and brown rice and pasta. Also try to cut down on fat, sugar and salt!

ACTIVITY

Plan a breakfast, lunch and evening meal suitable for a teenager, using the three empty plates below. Check to see you have the right number of portions of each food group!

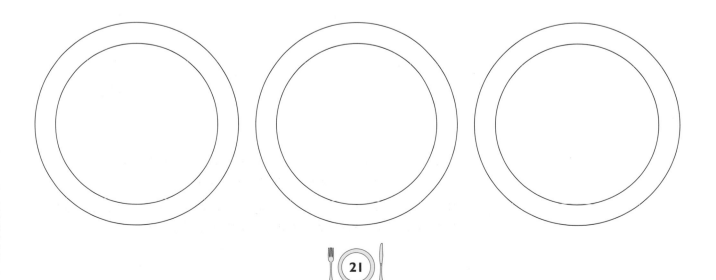

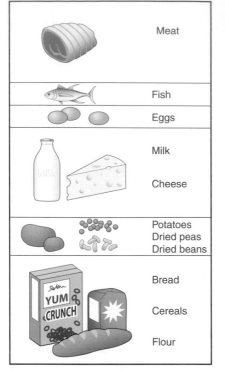

Sources of protein

More about nutrients – the 'science bit'

Protein

Protein is the most important nutrient. This is because it is the only nutrient that can be used for growth (so especially important for children) and the building and repair of body cells. Protein is also known as the 'body-builder'.

Protein can come from animals (fish, meat and animal products like cheese, milk and eggs) or plants (peas, beans and lentils – sometimes called pulses, soya, nuts and cereals).

There are two types of protein – proteins of high biological value (HBV) and proteins of low biological value (LBV). Proteins are made up of amino acids. HBV proteins contain the essential amino acids. Ten essential amino acids are needed by children and eight are needed by adults. HBV proteins are found in fish, meat, cheese, milk, eggs and soya. LBV proteins are found in peas, beans, lentils, nuts and cereals.

> **REMEMBER**
>
> Soya is the only plant-HBV protein. This is important to remember when planning meals for vegetarians and vegans.

Carbohydrates

Carbohydrates come from plants. They are the main 'energy providers'. They can be:

- starches e.g. cereals, bread, pasta, rice, potatoes, etc., or
- sugars e.g. sugar, honey, jams, marmalades, fruit, etc.

Fibre is sometimes classed as a carbohydrate – but more about that later!

Carbohydrates (starches and sugars) break down to simple sugars as they pass through the digestive system. Complex carbohydrates (such as whole grains) help maintain stable blood sugar levels. Too much sugary food in one go can affect blood sugar levels, making us feel energetic quickly, but then tired. Excess sugar is stored in muscle cells (to be

Sources of carbohydrates

ready for action) and in the liver. Unfortunately, if it is not used it is then stored as body fat.

Fats and oils

The first bit is easy to remember – fats are solid at room temperature and oils are liquid at room temperature. Examples of fats include butter, margarine, lard and dripping. Examples of oils include corn oil, sunflower oil, peanut oil and sesame oil.

Fats, like carbohydrates, are 'energy providers'. Because fats help to form an insulating layer under the skin they also give 'body warmth'. It is important to note that the same weight of fat gives twice as many calories as carbohydrates, so it is easy to eat too much! Although we hear a lot about how fat is 'bad for you', that's not quite true. Too much is bad for us, but our bodies need some fat for building cell membranes and for other jobs, like insulation.

However, we all need to make sure we don't eat too much fat. Too much fat can cause:

- obesity
- high cholesterol (fatty bits which clog the arteries)
- coronary heart disease (CHD)
- halitosis (bad breath)
- Type 2 diabetes.

Vitamins

Vitamins are only needed in tiny amounts by the body, but as the name suggests, they are vital for good health.

The main vitamins are named after letters of the alphabet. They all have chemical names as well – but you don't need to remember them! Every vitamin has a specific job to do in the body so a lack of one particular vitamin can make you feel a bit 'under the weather'.

Vitamin A is needed to make 'visual purple' in the eye, which is needed to prevent 'night blindness'. It is also needed to keep our mucous membranes (like the tissues found in the nose) moist.

Vitamin B is not one vitamin but a group of vitamins that includes thiamine, niacin and riboflavin. They are needed to help release the energy from carbohydrate foods.

Sources of fats

Good points about fats:

- They are needed to build cell membranes.
- They are needed to protect body organs e.g. the kidneys.
- They 'lubricate' or 'grease' food to make it easier to swallow.
- They make you feel full for a long time.
- They form an 'insulating layer' under the skin to keep the body warm.
- They give food a lovely flavour.
- They give food a good texture e.g. fried foods are often crisp.
- They contain the fat-soluble vitamins – particularly A and D.

A source of vitamin A

Vitamin C – does 'an apple a day keep the doctor away'? It's more likely to be an orange, some strawberries or blackcurrants! Vitamin C really is a vital vitamin. It is needed to make the connective tissue (a bit like glue) which holds body cells together. It also helps the body absorb iron. Have you ever wondered why visitors take fruit to people in hospital? Most accidents and operations involve loss of blood, so eating iron-rich foods with fruit containing vitamin C helps the body recover more quickly!

Vitamin D works with calcium to help form strong bones and teeth. Vitamin D is sometimes called the 'sunshine vitamin' because it can be manufactured (made) in the body by the action of sunlight on the skin. Don't overdo the sun though – burning can contribute to skin cancer.

Minerals

Gruesome fact: the mineral content of a body is all that is left after cremation, i.e. the ashes. Minerals are found in most foods and the only ones that might be lacking are calcium and iron. You need to know about these.

Iron is needed for making red blood cells. Blood is the body's transport system – it takes oxygen round the body to where it is needed. If there is not a good supply of red blood cells the transport system does not work very well. Lack of iron causes a disease called anaemia. This disease is more common in teenage girls and women because of monthly periods.

Sources of iron and calcium

Calcium is needed for strong bones and teeth. Calcium works with vitamin D and phosphorus. Calcium also helps the blood to 'clot'. It is important that children have enough calcium because most 'bone mass' is laid down before the age of about 21. Lack of calcium could cause osteoporosis (brittle bone disease).

Water

Do you know how much of your body weight is water? The answer is approximately 65 per cent. The body can survive a long time without food but only a couple of days without water. This is because many body 'processes' need water.

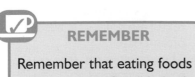

REMEMBER

Remember that eating foods rich in vitamin C will help the body absorb and make use of iron.

Water is needed to:

- help control body temperature
- lubricate (grease) joints
- help digestion
- help remove waste products from the body.

Adults need about $2\frac{1}{2}$ litres of water a day. About $1\frac{1}{2}$ litres comes from drinks. The rest comes from food. Fruits can be up to 90 per cent water – another good reason to eat five a day!

Fibre (NSP)

Fibre is also known by other names such as 'roughage' and 'non-soluble polysaccharides' (NSP) – what a mouthful! Fibre is not absorbed by the body – you can eat as much of it as you like and not put on any weight.

To understand why fibre is needed by the body, you need to imagine it passing through the body collecting all the rubbish and waste as it goes until it is finally 'expelled' from the body as faeces. As fibre passes through the body it absorbs water and bulks up the waste, making it soft. Lack of fibre can cause constipation.

If waste products stay in the intestines too long they can cause problems. Doctors think some cancers can be caused by lack of fibre and recommend that we eat 30g fibre a day. Fresh fruit and vegetables are high in fibre – yet another reason to eat five a day!

Malnutrition

Some diseases are caused by not having enough nutrients (starvation or under-nourishment) or by eating too much or too little of one or more nutrients (malnutrition).

ACTIVITY
Look at the sentences below and fill in the blank spaces correctly, using a word from the following list: fat, carbohydrates, protein, vitamin A, vitamin B, vitamin C, vitamin D, iron, calcium, water, fibre.

Be careful – some nutrients are used more than once!

_____ is not a nutrient but is needed for healthy bowels and to avoid constipation.

> **KEY FACTS**
> - Eat less sugar to prevent dental caries.
> - Eat less fat to prevent obesity.
> - Eat less fat to prevent coronary heart disease.
> - Eat less salt to prevent high blood pressure.
> - Eat more fibre to prevent constipation and bowel cancer.

Blood needs _____ to make red blood cells, which carry oxygen around the body to where it is needed.

Muscles in the body need _____ for work and physical activity.

_____ helps the body burn up energy foods..

Teeth need _____ and _____.

Two-thirds of your body weight is _____. It helps your body to function properly.

Eyes need _____.

Bones need _____ and _____.

Every cell of the body needs _____ for growth and repair.

The cells of the body must be held together. Body cells need _____ to be able to do this.

_____ is also needed to prevent illness. _____ keeps the body warm and gives us energy. Too much _____ can cause obesity.

How does eating 'five a day' of fruit and veg fit into healthy eating guidelines?

Healthy eating

'Five a day' fruit and veg

FOOD PREPARATION SKILLS

Throughout the course you will have plenty of opportunities to learn new practical skills. The following is a guide to the level of skill needed to prepare dishes. You should aim to develop for the higher-level skills and use them when you carry out practical work or take part in functions.

Skills and presentation

Higher-level skills:

- Pastry making – short crust, pate sucre, choux.
- Roux-based sauces.
- Meringues and pavlovas.
- Meat and fish cookery (using high-risk foods)
- Decorated cakes and gateaux.
- Rich yeast doughs.
- Complex accompaniments and garnishes.

Fish is a high-risk food

Medium-level skills:

- Basic bread doughs.
- Simple cakes, biscuits, cookies and scones.
- Vegetable and fruit dishes requiring even sizes e.g. fruit salad, stir-fries that show competent knife skills.
- Cheesecakes and similar desserts.
- Simple sauces e.g. red wine sauce.
- Puff pastry items that need shaping but use ready-made pastry.

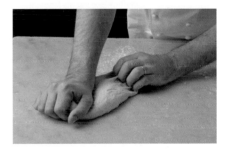

Basic skills:

- Assembling products e.g. using prepared sauces, bought meringue nests etc.
- Crumbles.
- Sandwiches.
- Pizza with ready-made base.
- Jacket potatoes.
- Simple salads.

Presentation:

- The finished appearance overall – the 'look' of the dishes when presented.
- Colour.

- Use of decoration and garnish.
- Correct texture or consistency of food.
- Flavour and seasoning.
- Temperature of food (hot or cold as appropriate).
- Correct serving dishes.

Preparing different foods

Meat and poultry

In the UK we eat the meat of three main animals. These are pigs, (ham, gammon, pork and bacon) sheep (lamb and mutton) and cows (beef and veal). We also eat poultry (chicken, turkey, goose and duck) and game birds such as partridge and pheasant. The edible internal organs of animals, known as offal, (liver, kidneys, heart etc.) are also eaten.

Most of the lamb we eat comes from animals that are less than six months old. Beef comes mainly from bullocks (male animals) because the females are needed for milk. Pork and bacon come from different types of pig – pork pigs tend to be short and fat. Bacon pigs are long and thin.

Meat is made up of long, thin muscle fibres held together with connective tissue. Some cuts of meat are tougher than others. Cuts of meat like shin beef come from the part of the animal that does a lot of work (i.e. the leg, in this case). For this reason, shin beef needs long, slow cooking like stewing. Other cuts of meat (e.g. fillet, sirloin or rump steak) can be cooked quickly because the muscle fibres are shorter.

Checking the temperature of meat

ACTIVITY

Suggest a different cooking method for each of the cuts of meat listed below. The cooking methods are given for you to choose from.

Meat: Pork chops, leg of lamb, pork fillet, neck of lamb chops, sirloin steak.

Methods: Stewing, frying, roasting, grilling, stir-frying.

Meat and poultry can carry bacteria that can cause food poisoning. They must be stored away from cooked foods. Frozen meat and poultry must be defrosted thoroughly before cooking. Take care when cooking meat and poultry – remember they are high-risk foods. Lamb and duck can be served 'pink' and beef can be served 'rare'. All other meat and poultry should be thoroughly cooked.

Fish

There are three types of fish:

- oily – salmon, tuna, sardines, mackerel, etc.
- white – cod, haddock, whiting, plaice, sole, coley, etc.
- shellfish – prawns, shrimps, scampi, crabs, mussels, oysters, etc.

The flesh of fish is made up of muscle and connective tissue. Because the muscles are short and the connective tissue is very thin, fish cooks very quickly. Fish of all types 'go off' quickly, so it is important to carry out quality checks. Fish should smell slightly salty or like the sea, it should have firm flesh, bright red gills and clear eyes with plenty of scales. Shellfish must have tightly closed shells and a fresh smell.

Fish is great to cook with because it cooks quickly and can be used in many different dishes. Remember to store it in the fridge until it is needed. Shellfish is a high-risk food so should be eaten on the day it is bought. Tinned (canned) fish is a very good alternative to fresh fish and provides excellent food value.

ACTIVITY

Match the fish in the list to the correct dish. You may need to use a recipe book, or ask your teacher to help.

Plaice	Chowder
Clams	Moules marinières
Tinned salmon	Rollmops
King prawns	Battered fish with chips
Cod	Kedgeree
Smoked haddock	Fish goujons
Herrings	Kebabs
Mussels	Fishcakes

Pasta, rice and other cereals

The main cereals are wheat, rice, corn, oats, barley and rye. They can be used as:

- grains – whole or crushed
- flour – to make pasta, bread, cakes, pastries, biscuits, etc.

- breakfast cereals – Shredded Wheat, Rice Krispies, cornflakes, porridge, etc.

Flour is used extensively in the catering industry. Different varieties of wheat produce different flours. Strong wheat has a high protein (gluten) content and produces strong flour, used for making pasta and bread. Weak wheat has a low protein (gluten) content and produces soft flour that is used for making ordinary baked goods like cakes, pastry and biscuits.

ACTIVITY

What type of flour would you use for:

- iced buns?
- wholemeal bread rolls?
- short-crust pastry?
- Swiss roll?
- fairy cakes?
- scones?

Rice and pasta make excellent alternatives to potatoes. Dried pastas, in particular, have all the advantages of rice. They:

- are cheap to buy
- are easy to obtain
- are easy to store
- have a long shelf life
- cook quickly
- have good nutritional value
- can be used in a number of different ways
- come in a variety of types.

ACTIVITY

Pasta comes in many different shapes and sizes e.g. spaghetti and ravioli. Name and describe six other shapes.

Rice is the grain of a cultivated grass. Chefs use different varieties of rice depending on the dish they are making. Short-grain rice 'clumps' together when cooked. Pudding rice (used for rice pudding) and arborio rice (used for risottos) are examples of short-grain rice. Long-grain rice remains fluffy, firm and separate when cooked, so is popular in dishes such as curry. Examples of long-grain rice are Carolina and basmati. Brown rice gives more food value than white rice but has a long cooking time. Wild rice is another grass that has a high nutritional value. It is expensive but makes food look attractive. It is sometimes mixed with other rice.

Fruit and vegetables

These are very useful in cookery because of their colour, flavour, texture and versatility. They are high in nutrients. Government nutritionists recommend that everyone should eat at least five portions a day of fruit and vegetables.

Fruit is best eaten fresh if possible. but other forms are useful additions to a balanced diet. Fruit can be:

- dried – e.g. dates, figs, currants, sultanas, raisins, apples, bananas, prunes
- canned (tinned) e.g. mandarin oranges, pears, peaches, pineapple, and mixed fruits (e.g. fruit cocktail)
- frozen e.g. apples, blackcurrants, raspberries, strawberries, mixed fruits
- made into juice e.g. oranges, apples, pineapples, blackcurrants, mixed tropical fruits, mixed citrus fruits, cranberries
- made into jam/preserves e.g. strawberries, raspberries, apricots, damsons, plums, mixed fruits, citrus fruits for marmalade, mango for mango chutney
- glacé (preserved in heavy sugar syrup) e.g. cherries
- crystallized (whole fruits preserved in sugar) e.g. peaches, mandarins, cherries
- candied (preserved in sugar) e.g. orange and lemon peel (mixed peel).

ACTIVITY
Name a different dish that you could prepare with each of the following types of fruit: frozen apples, glace cherries, orange juice, tinned pineapples, sultanas, apricot jam.

Vegetables are traditionally used for savoury dishes, while fruits are used for sweet dishes. The 'fruits' of a plant always contain the seeds, stone or pips of a new plant (with a few exceptions e.g. rhubarb). Vegetables can come from any part of a plant. If you picture a vegetable in your mind it will help you identify which part of the plant you are preparing and eating.

Here are some examples of types of vegetables;

- roots – carrots, parsnips, turnips, beetroot
- tubers – potatoes and Jerusalem artichokes
- bulbs – onions, shallots, garlic
- stems – asparagus, celery
- leaves – cabbage, lettuce, spinach, Brussels sprouts, spring greens

- flowers – cauliflower, broccoli
- seeds – peas, beans, sweetcorn
- fungi – mushrooms,

Peppers, tomatoes, courgettes, cucumber, marrow are all actually fruits, but we refer to them as vegetables and use them in savoury dishes.

One of the most important skills you will learn in catering is how to prepare standard vegetable cuts. Practice is essential in order to gain this skill. Good luck!

> ### ACTIVITY
> Draw diagrams of the standard vegetable cuts, then check them against the diagrams below.
>
> 1. julienne (matchsticks)
>
> 2. brunoise (tiny dice cut from julienne)
>
> 3. jardinière (batons)
>
> 4. macédoine (medium dice)
>
> 5. paysanne (triangles, circles, squares, crescents)

Julienne **Brunoise** **Jardinière** **Macédoine** **Paysanne**

Eggs

We can eat eggs from hens, turkeys, geese, ducks, guinea fowl, quail and gulls. The most commonly used are hens' eggs. They are graded in four sizes: small, medium, large and very large. The size of the egg only affects the price, not the quality. We can get free-range or battery eggs. When buying eggs you should look for:

- clean, well-shaped eggshells
- a high proportion of thick egg white to thin egg white when the egg is broken (a lot of thin egg white means the egg is old)
- yolks that are firm, round and an even colour.

Eggs are high in protein and they provide energy, fat, minerals and vitamins. They should be stored in a cool place.

The shells are porous and will absorb strong flavours, so they should be kept away from strong-smelling foods like onions. They can be fried, scrambled, poached, boiled or used in omelettes and a range of other dishes such as quiche.

Eggs are extremely versatile and can also be used in a variety of other ways:

- whisked – Swiss roll, sponge flan or gateau
- as a glaze – pastry dishes e.g. sausage rolls or pasties
- to set a mixture – quiche
- to bind – fish cakes
- to coat – fish cakes, chicken joints, scotch eggs
- to emulsify – mayonnaise.

Cheese

Cheese can be made from cows' or goats' milk. Most cheeses made in the UK are from cows' milk. Cheese is high in protein. It is also high in fat. Cheese can be hard, soft or blue veined. It should be stored in a cool place and wrapped. Buy cheese in small quantities as it doesn't keep for long.

Cheese can be eaten raw and there is very little, if any, waste. Some types have a wax coating that needs to be cut off. Cheese is fairly cheap, has good flavour and can be used in cooking e.g. sauces, cheesecakes, pasties.

ACTIVITY

List as many cheeses as you can think of in the following categories:

- hard
- soft
- blue.

Describe six different ways of using cheese in cooking.

Tofu with mushrooms and salad

Vegetable protein

Some people prefer not to eat produce from an animal and use alternatives such as textured soya (mince or pieces), quorn, or tofu. Textured soya is a protein made from wheat and soya beans. It can also be used as a meat extender: it can be used to replace as much as 60 per cent of meat in products such as meat pies. Quorn is produced from a plant derived from the mushroom family and can also be used as an alternative to meat; it does not shrink in cooking and can take on the flavour from the other ingredients it is cooked with. Tofu is made from soya beans and can be used in stir-fries and other dishes. It is high in protein.

Sauces

A sauce is a liquid that has been thickened.

The usual ways of thickening sauces are by using:

- a roux – equal quantities of fat and flour
- cornflour or arrowroot – blended to a paste with liquid
- beaten egg yolks.

A good sauce should be smooth, shiny and well seasoned. Sauces are used for many reasons. Here are some of the main ones. They:

- add colour
- add flavour/taste – especially to insipid (tasteless) food
- add texture
- bind (stick) foods together
- improve appearance or presentation of food
- add food value
- counteract (take away) the richness of some foods.

Sauces have different consistencies, depending on what they are being used for. A pouring sauce would be used for custard to accompany apple pie. A coating sauce would be used for cheese sauce to 'coat' cauliflower or macaroni. A really thick sauce called a 'panada' would be used to bind together the ingredients for fish cakes or meat balls.

Hot and cold desserts

There are many types of hot and cold desserts. Desserts can be made to suit all needs and tastes. Here are some examples:

- Egg-based desserts include crème caramel, bread-and-butter pudding and baked egg custard. In these dishes the eggs coagulate to enable the dessert to set.
- Steamed puddings are quite stodgy and heavy. They include jam roly-poly, treacle sponge and Christmas pudding. Traditionally they were served with custard, but can also be served with a sweet sauce or ice cream.
- Meringue-based products include Pavlova, vacherin and baked Alaska.
- Milk puddings can be eaten hot or cold and include baked rice pudding or semolina.

Desserts can be served with a range of sweet sauces including custard, almond sauce, Melba sauce, rum sauce or brandy butter.

Pastry products can be made from convenience mixes such as short crust. Using these products gives the chef more time to produce more dishes. You can also buy frozen pastry, such as short-crust or puff pastry, suitable for making a range of desserts. Pastry desserts include apple pie, profiteroles, lemon meringue pie, fruit tartlets and cream horns.

A lot of desserts include fresh fruit and can look very appealing to the eye. Although they may be high in fat and sugar it is possible to reduce these by using low-calorie sweeteners and unsaturated fats to meet the needs of those trying to live a healthier lifestyle.

> **ACTIVITY**
>
> List five dishes that can be made with whisked eggs.
>
> List five different types of pastry.
>
> Name four hot puddings that are baked.
>
> List six cold desserts using pastry.
>
> Find a recipe for ice cream and have a go at making it.
>
> Try the traditional way of cooking a steamed sponge pudding in a saucepan of water.

Basic dough products

Dough products are made from a basic bread dough containing yeast. To make basic bread dough, you should use strong plain flour as it contains more gluten. Gluten is a sticky protein found in wheat and other grains. When mixed with water, it becomes stretchy and helps the products to rise. The yeast in the dough is activated with warm water. It is killed by excess heat, and if this happens the dough will not rise. You can use quick-acting dried yeast or fresh yeast to make dough. Fresh yeast is not always available and dried yeast can be stirred straight into the flour, it does not need to be mixed with water first. Oil or fat is added to keep the dough fresh, but it is not essential. Salt is also added to give the dough more flavour.

Kneading the dough helps to stretch the gluten so that the dough can rise and keep its shape. It can be done by hand or machine, using a dough hook. A food processor can also be used for small quantities. The dough should then be left to rise in a warm place. It should be loosely covered to prevent a hard skin forming. The dough should be baked in a hot oven Gas 8, 230°C – the heat makes the bread rise a little more before killing the yeast, and the bread then sets and holds its shape. The bread can be brushed with beaten egg and milk to give it a glazed finish. To test if bread is ready, tap the bottom. If it sounds hollow it is cooked.

A basic bread dough can be shaped in many ways e.g. loaf, plait or knot. Toppings such as seeds or cheese can be added to give the dough more flavour and texture. Ingredients can be added to the dough to give it more flavour, such as; currants, herbs or garlic.

ACTIVITY

Find out the names of a variety of breads from four other countries.

Make a sweet product from a basic bread dough.

Make a flavoured dough and shape it. How does it change during cooking?

ACTIVITY

Fill in the missing words to show how to make a basic dough.

Mix _____ and fat in a bowl. In a jug, mix _____ , salt and _____ together. Gradually add _____ mixture to _____ to form a soft, but not sticky dough. _____ until smooth, _____ and leave to rise. Cook at Gas 8, 230°C until bread is firm and brown. If the bottom sounds _____ when tapped, the bread is ready.

Cakes, sponges, scones and biscuits

There are four different methods of making cakes, sponges, scones and biscuits:

- the rubbing-in method
- creaming
- whisking
- melting.

The rubbing-in method is used for cakes, scones, pastry and some biscuits. It is used for cakes that do not have a large amount of fat compared to flour e.g. rock buns which have 75g fat and 200g flour.

- The fat is cut into chunks (block margarine is best) and, using the fingertips, is rubbed into the flour to form crumbs.
- Any optional ingredients (e.g. sultanas) are then added before the liquid or egg that binds the crumbs together.
- The mixture is baked in a fairly hot oven, Gas 5 or 6 (190°–200°C). The cakes will only keep fresh for a short time as they do not contain a lot of fat.

The creaming method is used for cakes that contain more fat and sugar compared to flour, such as sponge cakes. These cakes will last longer as they have more fat than those made using the rubbing-in method.

- The fat and sugar are creamed together using a wooden spoon. The eggs and flour are then added and mixed to make a light and fluffy mixture.
- Self-raising flour is used to make the cakes rise and so there is no need to add baking powder.
- It is better to use soft margarine for these cakes as it is easier to cream. Caster sugar has smaller crystals than granulated, so it mixes better. Flavourings such as cocoa can be added to the mixture.
- The eggs should be at room temperature.
- These cakes are cooked at a lower temperature, Gas 4 or 5 (180°– 190°C) for 20–25 minutes.

The whisking method is used for making light sponge cakes. This type of cake does not contain any fat, so does not keep well.

- The eggs and sugar are whisked together until they are light and you can form a figure eight on top.
- The self-raising flour is sieved and folded into the

mixture gently using a metal spoon. This must be done a little at a time to prevent pockets of flour forming.

● The mixture is then put into the prepared tins and cooked at Gas 6 (200°C) for 10–12 minutes. The mixture is very light and flexible making it ideal to roll when warm.

● It can be decorated in a variety of ways with fresh cream and fruit.

The melting method is used less often than the other methods. The fat and syrup are melted in a pan and poured into the other ingredients. The mixture is very wet and these cakes often improve in flavour if kept a little.

ACTIVITY

List four cakes that can be made using the rubbing-in method.

Try making a cake using the creaming method.

Make and decorate a gateau using the whisking method.

Find three recipes for cakes using the melting method. Put these recipes into your recipe file to try at a later date.

Scones and biscuits are often made using the rubbing-in or creaming methods. Scones are easy to make and take only a short time to cook. As they do not contain a lot of fat, they should be eaten soon after being made. Scones should be light, well risen and golden brown. The scone dough should be soft not sticky, the scones should be 2 cm thick before they are put in the oven and they should be cooked at the top of a hot oven. Do not over handle the scone mix as it will make the scones heavy and hard.

Biscuits are easy to make at home and have a better flavour than shop-bought biscuits. You should always leave the biscuits on the tray to cool after cooking, as this will give them time to set a little. Biscuits do not set until they are cool, so don't leave them in the oven until they are crisp.

ACTIVITY

Find a recipe for biscuits using the creaming method and another using the rubbing-in method. Try them out and compare the results.
Make sweet and savoury scones.

Make shortbread biscuits, using the basic ingredients listed in the box. Then change the ingredients to see what happens. Compare your results as a class.

✓ **REMEMBER**

Remember, some biscuit mixtures will spread when cooking so leave a space around the mixture. Grease the tray well to prevent the biscuits from sticking.

BASIC INGREDIENTS FOR SHORTBREAD:

150g plain flour
100g butter
50g caster sugar

Then try one of these ingredients instead:
– self-raising flour or wholemeal flour
– half butter, half lard or all lard
– brown sugar.

Culinary terms

Culinary terms are often used in professional kitchens and in recipes. Some are used more often than others. Below are some of the terms you will be expected to know by the end of your course.

Term:	Meaning:
accompaniments	Items offered separately to main dish.
al dente	Firm to the bite.
au gratin	Sprinkled with cheese or breadcrumbs and browned.
bain-marie	A container of water to keep foods hot without fear of burning.
brûlée	Burned cream.
bouquet garni	A small bundle of herbs.
coulis	Sauce made of fruit or vegetable puree.
croutons	Cubes of bread that are fried or grilled.
en croûte	In pastry.
entrée	Main course.
flambé	To cook with flame by burning away the alcohol.
garnish	Served as part of the main item, trimmings.
julienne	Thin, matchstick-size strips of vegetables.
marinade	A richly spiced liquid used to give flavour and assist in tenderising meat and fish.
mise-en-place	Basic preparation prior to assembling products.
purée	A smooth mixture made from food passed through a sieve.
reduce	To concentrate a liquid by boiling or simmering.
roux	A thickening of cooked flour and fat.
sauté	Tossed in fat.

KEY WORD

Mise-en-place – basic preparation prior to assembling products.

REMEMBER

Always complete your basic preparation prior to cooking and you will find your practical tasks much easier to complete. Preparation is important!

Presenting food

The aim of a chef is to present food as near perfectly as possible. This involves taking into account:

- consistency (how thin or how thick)
- texture (includes crunchy, soft, crisp)
- flavour (includes salty, sweet, sour, bitter, well seasoned)
- seasoning (includes use of herbs, spices, salt and pepper)
- colour (remember white, cream, brown and green are 'dead' colours)
- decoration (used on sweet dishes – includes chocolate, cherries, fresh fruit etc)
- garnish (used on savoury dishes – includes tomato, parsley, lemon, cucumber, cress, etc.)
- accompaniments – these include colourful vegetables and sauces.

Chefs gradually learn the skills of tasting food to check for flavour, texture and seasoning.

Hot foods should be served hot and *not* warm, preferably on hot plates. Cold food should be served cold, but *not* frozen and always on cold plates. Food probes can be used to check temperatures.

Savoury food is usually served in oval dishes or on oval plates if appropriate (with plain doilies or dish-papers)

Sweet food is usually served in round dishes or on round plates if appropriate (with pretty doilies).

Consistency

The consistency of food will depend on the size of pan used, the cooking time, the amount of thickener (e.g. flour) used and the quality of ingredients. It is easier to thin a mixture (like a soup or a sauce) rather than thicken it.

Texture

Tasting food is essential in order to test texture. This includes checking foods like rice, pasta (cooked al dente), and vegetables to ensure they are not over-cooked. Cooking alters the texture of food and an experienced cook will know when the right amount of heat has been applied to give the correct texture, for example when

REMEMBER

As a general rule, do not over season, over-decorate or over-fill serving dishes.

40

cooking steaks. Contrasting textures are important to give variety and interest to a meal, for example croutons with soup, wafers and ice-cream, cheese and biscuits.

Flavour and seasoning

Taste is very important. Good chefs know how to retain the flavour of food and how to alter the flavour of food. To retain flavour, chefs need to:

- use food that is as fresh as possible
- use the least amount of cooking liquid
- use left-over cooking liquid where possible (for sauces, stocks and gravies)
- use appropriate cooking methods
- prepare, cook and serve in as short a time as possible
- avoid over-seasoning, so that the natural flavour comes through
- use herbs and strongly flavoured foods with care
- adjust seasoning at the end.

Food poisoning

What is food poisoning?

Food poisoning is an illness you get by eating contaminated food. Food is contaminated if there is something in it which should not be there, things like bacteria and other microbes (viruses, moulds).

Other causes of food poisoning include:

● eating food that contains chemicals and metals.
● eating poisonous plants (e.g. toadstools, berries).

High-risk foods

Bacteria really like foods that are moist and high in protein. These include:

● meat
● poultry
● eggs
● stocks
● shellfish
● cooked rice.

● fish
● dairy products
● gravies
● sauces
● seafood

Why bacteria make us ill

Some bacteria have to be inside your body to make you ill. Once inside you, the bacteria attack your body causing illness. Some produce a toxin (poison) on the food which makes you ill when you eat it.

How bacteria multiply

Bacteria reproduce rapidly by dividing in two, which is known as binary fission.

Each bacterium only needs 10–20 minutes to multiply.

● 1 bacterium = millions in a few hours.
● ideal conditions for growth: food + moisture + warmth +time.

Shellfish

Cooked rice

SYMPTOMS OF FOOD POISONING

Abdominal pain – pain in the abdomen (stomach-ache)
Diarrhoea – 'the runs'
Vomiting – being sick
Nausea – the feeling of sickness
Fever – a raised temperature

Symptoms vary depending on the type of food poisoning and can last for days.

Critical temperatures

High-risk and perishable foods should be kept out of the danger zone temperatures of between 5°C and 63°C.

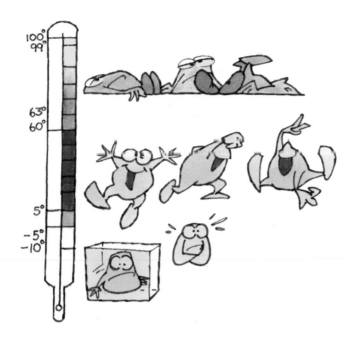

TYPES OF FOOD POISONING BACTERIA	

Campylobacter	• Found in raw poultry and meat.
	• Illness caused by small numbers of bacteria.
	• Symptoms:
	  – fever
	  – headache
	  – abdominal pain
	  – diarrhoea
	  – can last for 10 days.

Salmonella	• Found in raw meat, unwashed vegetables, poultry and eggs.
	• Second most common cause of food poisoning.
	• Survives refrigeration.
	• Illness caused by large numbers of bacteria.
	• Symptoms:
	  – fever – can be fatal!
	  – diarrhoea – can take up to 48 hours for
	  – vomiting symptoms to show.
	  – abdominal pain. – can last for 3 weeks.

E Coli 0157	• Found in the gut of animals and humans.
	• E Coli 0157 is found in raw and undercooked meats, raw vegetables.
	• Illness caused by small numbers of bacteria.
	• Can survive refrigeration and freezing.
	• Symptoms:
	– diarrhoea – can be fatal.
	– can take up to 5 days for symptoms to show.
Clostridium Perfringens	• From animal faeces.
	• Found in soil, manure, sewage, raw meat and poultry.
	• Produces spores which may not be killed by cooking.
	• Symptoms:
	– abdominal pain
	– diarrhoea
	– nausea
	– can be fatal
	– onset normally after 8–18 hours.
Listeria	• Found in soil, vegetation, meat, poultry, soft cheese, salad vegetables.
	• Can grow at low temperatures.
	• Symptoms:
	– range from flu-like symptoms to meningitis
	– pregnant women, the very old and the very young are most at risk
	– can take up to weeks to develop.
Bacillus Cereus	• Found in soil and dust.
	• Frequently in rice dishes and sometime in pasta, meat or vegetable dishes.
	• Illness can be caused by a small number of bacteria.
	• Forms spores that are resistant to heat.
	• Symptoms (two types of illness):
	– diarrhoea, abdominal pain after 8–18 hours
	– vomiting after 1–5 hours
	– usually lasts less than 24 hours.
Staphylococcus Aureus	• Found on the skin, in cuts and boils and up the nose.
	• Transferred to food from hands, nose or mouth.
	• Large numbers needed to cause illness.
	• Survives refrigeration.
	• Produces a toxin which may survive cooking.
	• Symptoms:
	– severe vomiting – onset within 6 hours
	– abdominal pains – lasts about 2 days.
	– diarrhoea

The 1995 Food Safety (General Food Hygiene) Regulations

Why do we have food hygiene regulations?

We have food hygiene regulations to prevent outbreaks of food poisoning.

Customers need to know that food is safe to eat. Food safety regulations are constantly changing and establishments should follow the latest guidelines. For example in 2006, regulations were updated and 'Safer Food Better Business' was introduced. Food safety and hygiene regulations are enforced by EHOs (environmental health officers) who regularly check all food premises.

What are the main requirements of the regulations?

The food hygiene regulations cover three main areas:

- food premises
- personal hygiene of employees
- hygienic practices.

Food premises

Food premises must:

- be well maintained
- be regularly cleaned
- have lockers for employees
- have hand-wash facilities provided
- have clean cloakroom and toilet facilities
- have first aid available
- have clean storage areas
- have temperature-controlled fridges and freezers
- have equipment that is clean and in good working order
- be free from pets, pests etc.

Personal hygiene of food handlers

Food handlers should:

- have regular training in food safety
- be dressed in clean 'whites' or other uniform

- have hair tied back (and ideally wear a hat)
- have short, clean nails – no nail varnish or jewellery
- be in good health (they cannot work with upset stomachs)
- have 'good' habits e.g. no coughing or sneezing over food,
- and wash their hands after handling raw meat, after blowing nose, after going to the toilet etc.

Cuts should be covered with blue waterproof plasters.

Hygienic practices

- Food deliveries should be checked thoroughly.
- Food should be labelled and stored correctly (in freezers, chillers, fridges and dry stores).
- Food should be 'rotated' (first in, first out).
- Care should be taken with temperature control in the kitchen (i.e. food kept out of the danger zone of 5°–63°C).
- Food should be prepared quickly and as close to cooking time as possible.
- Hot food should be maintained at above 63°C.
- The core temperature of cooked food needs to be at least 75°C.
- Chilled food should be stored below 5°C.
- Washing up should be done in hot soapy water if there is no dishwasher available.
- Waste should be disposed of safely.

ACTIVITY

Give five reasons why safer food leads to better business.

Find out what qualifications are available in food safety and hygiene.

Find out about the role of the EHO.

A temperature probe

Food handling

High standards of personal, food and kitchen hygiene are needed to keep food safe and prevent food poisoning.

What do we mean by personal hygiene?

Good personal hygiene means ensuring that germs found in or on the body do not transfer to food. We need to have high standards of personal hygiene or cleanliness.

KEY WORDS:

EHO: Environmental Health Officer
Regulations: Legal requirements
Core temperature: The temperature in the middle of the food

PERSONAL APPEARANCE OF KITCHEN STAFF

Long hair tied back

Discreet make-up

Neckerchief to absorb
sweat from neck

Nails short and clean
No nail varnish

No jewellery (except wedding ring)

No heavy perfume, scent or
aftershave

Cuts covered with
blue waterproof plasters

Loose-fitting trousers

Flat, comfortable shoes non-slip
with protective toe caps for kitchen

No facial piercing

Wearing of hat

Clear complexion

Daily shower or bath

No body odour (B.O.)

Correct clean uniform

No illness or stomach
complaints

Chefs should:

- wash hands before handling food
- wash hands when changing from one food to another
- wash hands after going to the toilet, blowing nose, smoking or handling waste
- have short clean nails
- cover cuts and sores with blue waterproof detectable plasters
- be in good health
- tie back long hair, or preferably cover it with a hat
- be dressed appropriately in clean clothes – 'whites'
- taste food with a clean teaspoon which is then washed.

Chefs should *not*:

- wear outdoor coats in the kitchen
- wear nail varnish, false nails or jewellery
- work when suffering from stomach upsets, sickness or diarrhoea
- smoke, eat or drink around the food
- cough or sneeze over food.

What do we mean by food hygiene?

Good food hygiene means ensuring food is safe to eat so that it does not give customers food poisoning.

Chefs should:

- store foods at the correct temperature (chilled food under 5° C, frozen food under -18° C)
- defrost frozen foods thoroughly before cooking
- keep food cool, clean and covered
- prepare food as close to cooking or serving time as possible
- take steps to prevent cross-contamination
- use colour-coded boards and knives
- separate raw and cooked foods
- prepare food on clean work surfaces
- sanitise work surfaces and equipment regularly
- adopt a 'clean-as-you-go' routine
- cook foods at a high enough temperature for a long enough time to kill bacteria
- use a temperature probe to check core temperature of food
- wash fruit and vegetables before use
- check 'use by' and 'best before' dates
- use pasteurised egg products, if appropriate, for 'high risk' dishes
- clean all equipment used in preparation of food thoroughly
- dispose of waste hygienically
- cool or chill food rapidly so that it is out of the danger zone (5° C to 63° C) where bacteria multiply rapidly
- re-heat food thoroughly (but do not serve to 'high risk' groups)
- refrigerate and cover food trolleys and buffets
- check fridge temperature at least three times a day.

Chefs should *not*:

- top up 'high risk' foods like mayonnaise on salad bars
- reheat food for 'high-risk' groups.

What do we mean by kitchen hygiene?

Good kitchen hygiene means ensuring kitchens are clean and well organised so that customers are not at risk of food poisoning.

Kitchens should:

● have a cleaning schedule

EXAMPLE OF A CLEANING SCHEDULE

What is to be cleaned?

Who will carry out the cleaning?

When the cleaning needs to be done (e.g. daily, weekly, monthly)?

How the cleaning is to be done (e.g. methods and standards)?

The time needed for the cleaning.

The cleaning materials to be used (chemicals, materials and equipment).

Safety precautions (e.g. wearing of gloves, goggles, etc).

Signature of person carrying out the cleaning, and signature of supervisor.

● have good ventilation, lighting and extraction fans if needed

● have clean well-ventilated food stores

● rotate stock so that the oldest stock is used first (damaged canned or packaged food should not be used)

● have freezers and fridges with visible temperature controls

● clean and check freezers and fridges regularly (out-of-date food should be thrown out)

● wash dirty pans, cutlery and crockery as soon as possible

● have designated hand-wash and cloakroom areas

● have floors, walls and work surfaces that are easy to clean and sanitise

● mop up spillages immediately

● wipe down surfaces regularly (do not allow food crumbs to accumulate)

● have high standards of waste disposal

● ensure that all bins are covered with lids so that vermin/pests cannot gain access

● have good pest control i.e. insect-o-cutors, window mesh etc.

● report cases of infestation of insects (flies, cockroaches) or rodents (rats and mice) immediately.

Damage caused by flies and rats

ACTIVITY

Look at the picture on the next page. If you were appointed as Head Chef, what would you need to do to ensure higher standards of food safety?

Accident prevention

A catering kitchen can be a dangerous place. Here are the main dangers and ways of preventing accidents in the kitchen.

Floors

Mop up spills immediately.

Keep floors clean and grease-free.

Do not leave equipment in 'pathways' used in the kitchen.

Repair damaged floor surfaces quickly.

Knives

Use the right-sized knife for the food you are cutting.

Keep handles clean and grease-free.

Keep knives sharp – blunt knives need too much pressure.

Do not leave knives on edges of chopping boards or tables.

Do not put knives in washing–up bowls or point up in a dishwasher.

Do not try to catch a falling knife.

Electrical equipment

Check machinery is in good working order.

Check electrical wires are not frayed or worn.

Do not handle electrical equipment with wet hands.

Check safety notices.

Assemble equipment correctly and use safety guards.

REMEMBER

Some machinery (electrical equipment) cannot be operated by people who are under 18.

Saucepans

Indicate hot handles by sprinkling flour on them.

Take care when moving or lifting heavy pans.

Use oven gloves or oven cloths.

Turn pan handles towards the back of the cooker.

Do not use wet cloths for hot pans.

Fryers

Do not fill above the fat level indicated (usually up to half full).

Do not put wet foods into fryers.

Lower food into fryer carefully.

Change fat regularly.

Foods

Be aware that fish bones and meat bones can cause cuts.

Be aware that frozen food can cause 'burns'.

Take care when opening and disposing of cans and jars.

Store raw and cooked foods separately.

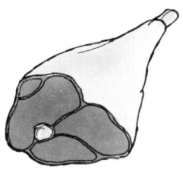

Storing equipment

Store all equipment safely e.g. knives in a knife block.

Unplug electrical equipment when not in use.

Replace safety guards on electrical equipment.

Fires

Do not have flames larger than the size of the pan.

Do not leave cloths or oven gloves over cookers.

Time the cooking of foods accurately.

Take special care when cooking in fat – it can spit and set alight.

Have fire blankets and fire extinguishers to hand.

Have clear fire procedures.

Clothing

Wear appropriate clothing in the kitchen.

Wear non-slip shoes or clogs.

Do not wear jewellery that can become trapped in machinery.

Tie long hair back. Cover hair with a hat.

Behaviour

Do not run in the kitchen.

Pay attention when given instructions or orders.

Concentrate on the job 'in hand'.

Make sure that workers are supervised at all times.

Cleaning

Try to 'clean as you go'.

Keep cleaning materials and equipment away from food areas.

Use the right cleaning materials for the task.

Do not 'mix' cleaning materials.

Use cleaning materials at the right strength.

Store cleaning materials and equipment carefully.

Accommodation areas can also be dangerous places. Here are the main dangers and ways of preventing accidents in accommodation areas.

Floors

Do not over-polish wooden floors.

Avoid the use of loose mats.

Have good lighting, especially where there are steps.

Check flooring regularly and replace frayed carpets and worn tiles before they cause accidents.

Mop up spills immediately.

Bedrooms

Have hot water at a 'safe' temperature to avoid scalds.

Have non-slip surfaces in baths and showers.

Check electrical equipment e.g. TVs, kettles, hairdryers etc. frequently. Replace frayed flexes.

Do not have trailing bed clothes.

Cleaning

Do not have trailing flexes when using cleaning machines.

Be aware of broken glass in rubbish.

Be aware of razors placed in rubbish.

Empty rubbish bins carefully and safely.

Use 'wet floor' notices on hard floors when cleaning.

Do not 'mix' cleaning materials.

Handle cleaning equipment and cleaning materials carefully.

Store all cleaning equipment and cleaning agents in a locked cupboard.

Hazard Analysis Critical Control Points (HACCP)

Food hygiene laws mean that *all* businesses should have a Hazard Analysis Critical Control Points (HACCP) system in place.

Food producers need to understand *how*, *why* and *where* food could become contaminated and then set out to prevent it from happening. The HACCP system helps them to do this.

Food producers (this includes hotel and restaurant owners, not just food manufacturers) need to:

● have an HACCP system in place
● draw up a flow chart of **each step** in the preparation of **each dish** – starting with the buying of ingredients and ending with sale to the customer
● **analyse each step** of the process to see what could go wrong and could result in a danger to the customer (dangers or hazards include bacteria, chemicals and foreign bodies)

- identify what can be done to **control the hazards** e.g. separate raw and cooked food to prevent cross-contamination, have high standards of personal hygiene to avoid contamination, use correct cooking times and temperatures to kill bacteria
- **set standards** (known as critical limits) for each control point. This will state the conditions that **must be met** to ensure food is safe to eat. These controls must be checked regularly. Records must be kept to show the controls are working.
- **review HACCP** whenever there is a change to a recipe or a new dish on the menu or a change of activity in the kitchen. Otherwise, HACCP must be reviewed once a year.
- keep all documentation and records safe.

Critical control points for catering		
Step	**Hazard**	**Action**
1 Purchase	High-risk foods such as cooked meat could be contaminated with food-poisoning bacteria when you buy them.	– Buy from a supplier with a good reputation. – Specify a maximum temperature for food when it is delivered.
2 Receipt of food		– Check that food looks, smells and feels right when it is delivered. – Check the temperature of food.
3 Storage	Food-poisoning bacteria could grow on high-risk foods and contaminate other food.	– Keep high-risk food at a safe temperature and wrapped up. – Label food with a 'sell-by' date and use it up by that date. – Rotate stock so that the oldest food is used up before the 'sell-by' date.
4 Preparation	High-risk food could be contaminated with food-poisoning bacteria. Bacteria could grow.	– Wash your hands before you handle food. – Don't keep food out at room temperature more than you have to. – Use clean equipment. – Use different equipment for high-risk foods and other foods. – Separate raw foods from cooked foods.
5 Cooking	Food-poisoning bacteria could survive during cooking.	– Cook chicken, rolled joints and re-formed meat such as burgers so that the thickest part reaches 75°C. – Sear the outside of other meat (such as steaks) before cooking.

6 Cooling	Surviving food-poisoning bacteria could grow. Bacteria could produce poisons.	– Cool food as fast as possible. – Don't leave food to cool at room temperature unless it's only for a very short time. For example, put rice into a shallow dish so that it will cool quickly.
7 Hot-holding (keeping food hot, e.g. in a self-service cafeteria)		– Keep food at 63°C or hotter.
8 Reheating	Food-poisoning bacteria could survive during reheating.	– Reheat food to 75°C or higher
9 Chilled storage	Food-poisoning bacteria could grow.	– Keep the storage temperature right. – Label high-risk foods with the correct 'sell-by' date.
10 Serving	Food-poisoning bacteria could grow, causing disease. Bacteria could produce poisons.	Serve cold food as soon as possible after you remove it from the fridge, so that it doesn't get warm. – Serve hot food quickly so that it doesn't cool down.

Adapted from Department of Health guidelines

HACCP CHECKLIST FOR BUSINESSES

1. Provide food hygiene training.
2. Remind staff of the importance of personal hygiene.
3. Get staff to report illnesses.
4. Always monitor food safety controls (temperature of fridges etc).
5. Know your suppliers and check all supplies on delivery.
6. Separate raw and cooked food.
7. Have adequate washing facilities.
8. Take measures to avoid cross-contamination (i.e. put up hand-wash notices, colour-coded boards and knives, cleaning charts, good cleaning schedules).
9. Maintain food temperature controls (i.e. avoid danger zone of 5° C to 63° C, serve chilled food under 5° C and serve hot food above 63° C).
10. Have an effective cleaning programme.

Unit 2 is assessed through event-based functions. You will need to complete a portfolio of evidence of two events that you have taken part in. These events can be completed as a group, as a class, or on your own. Your teacher will tell you when the events will take place and may even give you the theme for the event.

You will need to include evidence of a range of key issues across the two events. The key issues are:

- front-of-house team
- accommodation operations
- restaurant service
- food and beverage service
- costing and portion control
- planning and preparation of meals
- event-based functions
- applying health and safety.

You will need to write up a record for each of the two events for your portfolio. You will be required to include an introduction to each event. In your introduction, it is a good idea to pick out the key words of the event and analyse them.

You should show a knowledge of the skills involved, although they may not all be needed in each event. The important thing is to show a range of your skills and knowledge from all the key issues across the two events.

Food for a summer event

You can, of course, run more than two events during your hospitality and catering course. You would then pick the best two to send in for your examination assessment. The advantage of doing it this way is that if you are absent for one of the events you will still have the chance to send in work.

> You **must** show that you have taken part in two events – this section is worth a lot of the marks and you can't afford to miss an event.

You may work in teams, but for assessment purposes you must produce an identifiable piece of individual work. This means that you can include some pieces of work done as a team, but you must also include work you have completed by yourself.

Key issues

Now let's look at each key issue in detail.

Front-of-house team

Front-of-house staff are the first people the customers come in contact with. First impressions are important, so front-of-house staff need to be well presented and friendly.

Skills within the front-of-house team include:

- administrative procedures – filing, processing enquiries
- billing of customers – methods of payment
- booking systems – procedures and recording
- communication – talking, listening, writing, reading, giving and receiving information
- customer care – welcome, body language, politeness
- ICT skills – data base, word-processing skills
- storage of personal data – governed by the Data Protection Act.

You will need to gain practical experience of these skills and show evidence of them in your portfolio. You might be able to use evidence from your role in one of your events.

Here are some of the ways you can collect evidence in a school or college situation:

- Keep a track of who is booked in at the event and record any enquiries from potential customers.
- How will the customers pay for the products – in advance or on the day? Keep a record of payments received and from whom.
- Bookings can be taken if places at the event are limited.
- You will show evidence of communication throughout your event as you will have to listen to others and act upon information received.
- Customer care can be shown in your write-up of the event as you can comment on how you made the customers welcome.
- ICT skills will be evident in your portfolio.
- Any personal information you received on customers should be protected (e.g. special requirements on the day can be recorded but the customer should not be identified).

Accommodation operations

You should show you have knowledge of the services provided by the accommodation team. This can be difficult

in a school/college environment, but you could include preparation for the function.

Let's look at the roles of the staff in this area:

- Conference/operations manager – organises the layout of the room and makes sure everything is available for the event.
- Room attendants/chambermaids – clean and service the rooms ready for the guests and prepare for meetings and functions.
- Housekeeper – prepares duty rotas, supervises and checks standards, deals with customer complaints in relation to their area of supervision.
- Linen/house porters – carries out heavy duties e.g. moving furniture, carrying customer's luggage, deliveries.
- Cleaners – carry out the daily general cleaning of the accommodation, special preparation and cleaning for function/business events.

To collect evidence in a school or college situation, you could include a plan of the room and describe how your group prepared it ready for the event.

- Did you have to set it up in a special way?
- Did you require tablecloths and napkins? If so, who prepared them?
- Did you have to move the furniture?

You could then explain that although your group did these jobs as the event was held in school/college, in the industry it would be the role of the accommodation staff.

ACTIVITY

In your group, imagine that you are the housekeeper in a family-run hotel. The hotel has 20 bedrooms. Draw up a rota for the staff showing which rooms need to be cleaned and have bedding changed over the space of a week. Five rooms are being used all week, there is a conference on Wednesday and new guests are arriving each day for the other bedrooms. There is also a function for 50 in the dining room on Saturday.

Restaurant service

In this section you could take on the role of one of the members of the restaurant team. You will need to show that you have an understanding of the roles and skills of the restaurant staff. Let's look at them in detail.

Restaurant manager

The restaurant manager leads the team. They plan and implement the ways in which the staff work as a team. They are responsible for helping the staff acquire the skills needed and attitudes required for the job, including organising training for staff. They have overall responsibility for the smooth running of the restaurant and its future development. They organise rotas and inform staff of any changes to the menu or number of customers.

Wait staff (waiters and waitresses)

The wait staff work as part of a team. They advise customers about the menus and take their orders. They prepare and clear tables, serve customers and play an important role in customer care.

For this role, you will also have to show a basic understanding of the layout of the restaurant, table-laying and waiting stations.

You could include:

- a plan of how you expect the room to look
- a plan of the table covers, showing appropriate cutlery etc.
- an explanation of why other areas in school/college are unsuitable for the event to be held there
- examples of napkin-folding
- an explanation of why restaurants have wait stations (e.g. to keep spare cutlery and crockery on/in).

ACTIVITY

Find out about the different ways of setting the table for the following:

- café service
- family dining
- special function
- breakfast.

Set the table up for these and take photos, or draw the designs, to show that you understand the differences.

A restaurant wait station

How to serve customers correctly

Before your guests arrive, make sure that all tables are set correctly and no cutlery is missing. Check that all knives

are facing inwards and that cutlery is straight. Are all the napkins set out correctly? Make sure that all the condiments are ready for the meal.

When your customers arrive, the first thing you should do is to make them welcome and show them to their seats. This is called 'greeting and seating'.

This is usually the restaurant manager's job. You will need to decide in your group who will take on this responsibility.

You may have a seating plan for your guests. This would also help when bringing the meals out, as you would know who had ordered what beforehand. Make sure that you stick to the seating plan, if you have one, to avoid disruption later.

You would then find out what the customers would like to drink. You would check if they have pre-ordered, and if they haven't, give them the menu. When you come back with the drinks you would ask if they are ready to order. Remember to be polite at all times. When you take the order you should stand to the left of the customer. You will need to be familiar with the menu and be prepared to answer any questions about the meal.

KEY WORDS

Wait staff: The waiters and waitresses are often referred to as 'wait staff'.
Greeting and seating: How the customers are met and taken to their table.
Seating plan: A plan of who will be sitting where on what table.

Taking out and serving the food

You should serve women and older people first. Always serve food from the left and clear from the right. However, drinks should be served from the right whenever possible. Always be polite. A few minutes after the meal, check that everything is OK with the meal after a few minutes. Remember to be attentive, but don't hover around the guests.

Food and beverage service

In this section you will need to show you understand:

- the types of service in relation to the types of establishment
- correct table layouts in relation to the type of menu and service
- how food is served differently for each type of menu
- the safe use, care and cleaning of food and beverage service equipment and why this is important.

REMEMBER

Serve from the left and clear from the right whenever possible.

Let's look at the different types of menu that are available.

Table d'hôte

This is a set menu for a set price. This type of menu may have a selection of starters, main course and dessert. The customer then selects which one they would prefer. There is usually a vegetarian option on the menu.

À la carte

This is a selection of courses, all priced individually and cooked to order. This menu usually has a wider choice for the customer for each course and may include a fish course and wider selection for vegetarians.

Take-aways

These menus give a list of various products (e.g. pizzas, Chinese) that are available at set prices. They are not eaten on the premises and may be delivered to the home.

Children's meals

Children's meals are often on a separate menu that is more colourful and may include a theme. The choices available are limited and often now include a healthier option or multiple choices so the parents can make up the meal to suit the needs of the child.

Set menu for a function

These menus usually have a choice for the customer and they may then chose one option for all guests or ask each guest what they require from a limited choice. These are often used for sit-down functions or for buffets where the clients choose the meal for a set price per person.

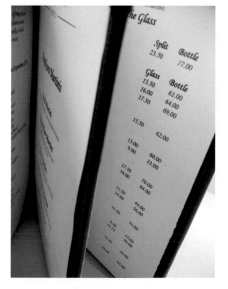

Fast food/café

These menus have a choice of quick-to-prepare foods at set prices. The foods may range from snacks, sandwiches and cakes, to a full dinner or breakfast. They also include drinks that can be bought alone or with the meal or snack.

Food and beverage service equipment

One of the main pieces of equipment used in the restaurant is the wait station. This is a unit with cupboards and drawers so you can store your spare cutlery and crockery, as well as any condiments you may need. It is a good idea to keep the top as clear as possible as this gives you somewhere to put the dirty equipment while you finish clearing the table. You would also keep spare folded napkins and menus, including children's menus, on here.

If you were in a restaurant taking orders you may have to use an electronic point of sale (EPOS). This is where you would take the order and enter it into the computer at your station. The order would then be transferred to the kitchen staff who would then prepare the order. At the end of service you would enter the customer's details and table number to get the bill. This system is becoming increasingly more popular as it avoids confusion and mistakes can be easily monitored.

This is something you could talk about in your portfolio and give examples of when and where it would be used.

Another piece of equipment you might use is the filter coffee machine. You would be trained on this in the restaurant as it is the wait staff's job to make and serve the coffee to the customers. This again is something you could add in your portfolio.

ACTIVITY

Observe different types of service in cafes and restaurants and discuss what you have learned with other members of your group.

Try folding napkins in different ways to see which one best suits your event.

Collect a range of menus and identify the following: à la carte, fast food, table d'hôte, vegetarian options.

Study a menu and identify the ingredients in each food item. Describe the method of cooking used. Suggest accompaniments to go with the food.

Practice serving customers correctly.

Customer service

In this section you should identify that you understand why customer satisfaction is important and how it can be measured. Your customers want to enjoy their experience and you want them to come back.

Sometimes you may have to handle guests with special needs or guests who are very young, elderly or disabled. Always do your best to meet the needs of these guests, just as you would any other. Make sure that older guests do not have to walk far to get to their table, if you can. Make sure that those who are disabled have enough room to move, especially if they are in a wheelchair.

If a customer complains, handle the situation calmly and courteously. Stay professional and never blame someone else. Remember the customer is always right.

This is good way to handle complaints:

- Listen to the details of the complaint.
- Repeat the complaint briefly to show you understand the problem.
- Handle the complaint promptly.
- Make an immediate adjustment if you can.
- Apologise.
- Always treat the customer in the way that you would like to be treated yourself.

Ways in which customer service can be measured

You will have to show that you can identify a range of methods of customer satisfaction. These could be either verbal or written feedback from the customer. For inclusion in your portfolio, you could have a questionnaire for customers to fill in or an evaluation sheet, or you could add letters of thanks from your guests. Remember to annotate these to say where they are from: don't just add them to your portfolio with no explanation. This would also be assessed as part of your evaluation.

Costing and portion control

During your events you will have to show you have knowledge of the basic principles of costing out meals, including overheads. You should show accurate costing out of your dishes and menus. It is important that you at least meet the costs of running your event and allow for any accidents on the day.

> **REMEMBER**
>
> Remember that all guests are equal and you should strive to treat them all in the same way. Handle each situation, no matter how unpleasant or unusual, with care and consideration.

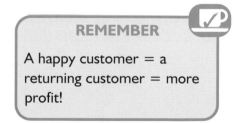

> **REMEMBER**
>
> A happy customer = a returning customer = more profit!

When costing your dishes you should include:

- how much the ingredients cost to buy
- how much of the ingredients you have used
- the cost of the amount you have used
- copies of till receipts or examples of costs from supermarket websites
- any special offers you get or ingredients that are free.

You could also include information on how much your overheads would be if you were in a restaurant or hotel. Overheads include electricity and gas, staff wages, wastage of foods. Most companies try to work on 60 per cent profit on the initial cost of the food to cover these.

Try to be as realistic as possible when you are costing out your event.

- Look at websites and compare prices for different supermarkets.
- Look for special offers.
- Buy in bulk whenever possible.
- Buy own brands as they are cheaper and often taste the same.

t	n	e	i	d	e	r	g	n	i
f	o	v	e	r	h	e	a	d	s
s	r	e	f	f	o	g	a	s	d
e	s	t	p	i	e	c	e	r	g
t	e	l	e	c	t	r	i	c	n
i	u	s	e	s	t	a	f	f	i
s	k	s	e	d	o	o	f	f	t
b	a	g	t	i	f	o	r	p	s
e	a	l	a	i	t	i	n	i	o
w	a	s	t	a	g	e	g	u	c

ACTIVITY

Find the following words in the grid:

ingredient, gas, wages, electric, staff, websites, food, offers. receipts, costing, profit, overheads, wastage.

You should show that you have an understanding of the need for portion control when carrying out your events. You should serve all the customers the same amount. You should show evidence that you have included good portion control when setting out your products. For example, if you are running a pizza event, your customers will all expect the same size pizza.

How can you achieve effective portion control?

- Use dishes that are the same size when cooking the product (e.g. pizza).
- Weigh the ingredients and allow a certain amount per person.
- Use plates that are the same size when serving the product.
- Use spoons that are the same size for serving the product.

- Show portion control in the decoration of a product e.g. gateau.
- Use scoops for ice cream or potatoes.
- Use ladles for soup and sauces.
- Use individual pie dishes.

You will have to decide in advance what size portions you will offer, you will then be able to work out how much of each product you will need. Remember that children and older people tend to eat less, and men tend to eat more than women, so take this into account when looking at your portion sizes.

Other things to take into consideration are:

- the quality of the food you buy – better quality usually yields a greater number of portions
- the buying price of the food, this should be relevant to the quality of the food you buy.

A portion of soup and bread

Planning and preparation of meals

You will be able to demonstrate a wide range of culinary skills in the preparation and serving of soups, starters, main courses, accompaniments, desserts and beverages across the two events. Using these skills you should be able to show that you can plan and present a variety of menus.

Things to consider when planning a menu

When choosing food for a menu you should consider:

- colour
- texture
- flavour
- the skills you have
- temperature
- time
- foods in season
- cost
- customer needs
- the occasion
- the type of menu.

You should show a range of skills across the two events. One event may only have a limited choice of foods available, e.g. pizza event. If this is the case you should

AS A GUIDE, YOU CAN GENERALLY ALLOW THE FOLLOWING:

- Soup – 4–6 portions per litre
- Meat – 6–8 portions per kg
- Cold meat – 16 portions per kg
- Potatoes – 8 portions per kg
- Vegetables – 6–8 portions per kg
- Sauces – 8–12 portions per 0.5 litre

An individual beef and onion pie

Chicken and vegetables provide different colours, flavours and textures

expand on your skills for the second event. That way you will be showing that you have gained a range of skills during the course.

Colour, flavour and texture

There is a saying that 'people eat with their eyes'. The food you present should look appetising to the customer. It should include a range of contrasting flavours, but not so many that you cannot taste the main product. Your complete meal should have a range of textures (e.g. smooth, crunchy).

Skills, temperature and time

Do not pick a recipe that you cannot realistically hope to make successfully. Your skills may not be developed enough yet. Also, think about the equipment you have available in the kitchen. Check the time it takes to cook the product and the temperatures. Remember you may have to use the oven for more than one thing at once, so check the temperatures for each product to see if it is possible to complete the meal.

Foods in season and cost

You will have to choose foods that are available and within your budget. Most foods are available all year now, but may be more expensive if they have been imported – for example, strawberries are cheaper to buy in June and July as they are available in this country. You will have to cost out your meal according to the ingredients you purchase.

Customer needs, occasion and type of menu

You will have to consider customers' needs and any special dietary requirements they may have. The type of occasion you are cooking for will affect the type of menu you have. For example, if you are holding a pizza event you will probably have a selection of three or four types of pizza available. If you are cooking a meal for a friend. you will have to think about their needs and tastes (e.g. it would not be appropriate to cook them a curry if they do not like spicy food).

Trialling your ideas

Always trial the recipes prior to the event. It is a good idea to select a range of recipes and try them out to see which one you can produce the best. By doing this you can also adapt recipes to suit your circumstances. Remember to try out the whole meal, not just parts of it, as you want to make sure you get the best results on the day.

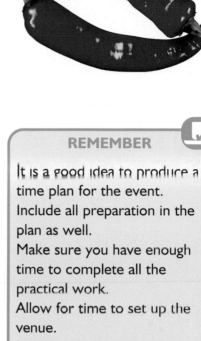

Event-based functions

Within your portfolio you will have to show that you have knowledge of the processes involved in organising a function. If you have worked through this section in the book you will already have completed most of the work, either individually or as a group.

> **THINGS TO CONSIDER WHEN PLANNING A FUNCTION**
> - the date and time of the event
> - the choice of venue and booking
> - the number of guests
> - the menu and type of service
> - costings
> - how you will promote the event
> - the décor and presentation
> - the room layout and table layout
> - the menu cards and place cards
> - reviewing the event.

Date and time of event

You will have to plan the event well in advance. Think about a date and time that is suitable for you, your school or college and your teacher as well as your guests.

Choice of venue and booking

You will have to think about where your event will be held and you may have to book the room. If you need a specific room (e.g. the hall) you will have to check that it is available and make sure that you book it with the relevant staff.

> **REMEMBER**
>
> It is a good idea to produce a time plan for the event.
> Include all preparation in the plan as well.
> Make sure you have enough time to complete all the practical work.
> Allow for time to set up the venue.
> Include job allocations for other members of the group.
> Take photographs of all practical work.

> You are invited to a
> *SPRING LUNCH*
> Albany School hall
> Tuesday 3rd April
> 12 o'clock
> **RSVP**

Number of guests

Be realistic about the number of guests you can cope with. If you only have a small group working on the event, you cannot cater for and serve a large number of guests. If you have already planned the time it will take to cook the food, remember that adding more guests will add more time.

Menu and type of service

The type of event you hold will determine the type of menu. You will also have to think about how you are going to serve the meal. Will it be plated before serving? Who is going to serve it? How will you serve the guests?

Costing

You will have to ensure that the prices you charge are relevant to the cost of the ingredients. See the section on costing and portion control to help you with this.

Promotion

How will you promote your event to your customers? You may start with a questionnaire asking people what sort of event they would like, or finding out if they would be interested in attending the event you have chosen. There is no point in holding an event if you have no customers! Could you put posters up around the venue prior to the event? What about personal invitations to special guests?

Décor and presentation

Does your event have a theme or colour scheme? For example, a pizza event venue could be decorated with Italian flags or have a red, green and white colour theme. How will you present your food?

Room layout and table layout

You will have to set up the room to suit the guests and the type of event. You will also have to think about the way you set the tables for the event. You can show evidence of this in your portfolio.

Menu cards and place cards

Are you going to have menus and place cards on the tables? If so, you could carry the theme through on both of these. Always try to complete the cards using ICT as you will get consistency and better quality in the end product. You want the customers to be impressed.

Reviewing

There may be occasions when you have had to change things for your event. This is not a problem – just make sure you annotate why the changes have been made in your portfolio.

Examples of events you could run

Your teacher might tell you what sort of event you will be holding, or you may be asked to think of something yourself. Let's look at some examples of the kinds of events you might be involved with.

Pizza café

You could work as a group to make a selection of pizzas to be sold at lunchtime to pupils and staff. The pizzas would be portioned and sold by the slice.

Coffee shop

As a group, you may be allocated a sum of money to run a coffee shop. You would decide what you make and sell to pupils and staff. Your event could take place at break or at lunchtime.

Meal for a friend

You could work individually to prepare, cook and serve a two-course meal for yourself and a friend.

Senior citizens' afternoon tea

Show your community spirit by planning and holding afternoon tea for a group of senior citizens. Link with the drama department and get them to organise entertainment.

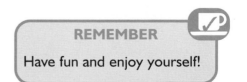

REMEMBER

Have fun and enjoy yourself!

Three-course meal for staff

As a group, you could prepare, cook and serve a three-course meal for a selected number of staff.

Gourmet meal for parents and staff

You could link with your local college of further education and use their training restaurant and kitchens to prepare and serve a gourmet meal for parents and staff.

These are just some examples of events you could hold. You may want to suggest other ideas to your tutor.

Applying health and safety rules

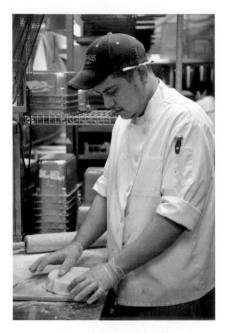

As well as holding your event, you should show how you would put HACCP (Hazard Analysis and Critical Control Points) into practice. You will need to construct a flow chart for the safe production of the foods, at all steps from delivery to consumption. You should show that you have knowledge of the common hazards in hospitality and catering outlets. (Look again at the section on HACCP.)

In your portfolio, you will need to include evidence that you have prepared the food safely. When preparing food, you will need to:

● use gloves to avoid cross contamination
● make sure that you wear protective clothing and a hat
● remove all jewellery
● cover cuts with blue plasters
● use the correct chopping boards.

Risk assessment

You will also have to show that you understand and can identify hazards that may occur during the event. You should be able to construct a risk assessment chart showing hazards and how they can be avoided.

Think about:

● fire procedures
● spills on floor
● cuts and burns
● wheelchair access if necessary
● using machinery

Quality check	Process	Hygiene risk
Check quality	Store food in fridge CCP	Bacterial growth
Check equipment not damaged	Collect equipment and ingredients	Bacterial growth
	Personal hygiene	Staphylococcus aureus or e. coli
Check date	Prepare and chop protein food (meat or chicken) on a red board CCP	Cross-contamination
Check freshness of vegetables	Prepare and chop vegetables on a green board	Cross-contamination Campylobacter from dirty vegetables
Not too much oil Visual check on meat changing colour	Put a little oil in the frying pan Add protein and cook until it seals	Salmonella from uncooked meat or poultry
Visual check on amount of sauce	Add vegetables and sauce	
Check more than one piece	Check core temperature of meat is at least 75°C	
Check wraps for consistency in size and shape	Prepare wrap Add salad	Campylobacter from soil on salad
Equal amount of filling in each Visual check for presentation	Add protein food and vegetables with sauce Serve while hot CCP	Bacterial growth if food is not served immediately

Example of an HACCP chart for a product made in a school or college

- carry equipment
- lifting heavy equipment
- reporting accidents.

ACTIVITY

When your event is over, check through and ensure you have covered all key issues within your portfolio. If there is anything you have missed, or cannot add because of the type of event you completed, make sure that you cover them in your next event.

Hazard	Who might be harmed?	Is the risk adequately controlled?	Further action required to control risk
Special dietary requirements	Customers	Staff have checked dietary requirements	Check that meals are OK before they are eaten
Fire	All	Fire procedure checked	Fire procedure gone over with pupils
Hazards relating to group activities, including cuts and burns	All	All safety procedures gone over with pupils	First aid kit carried Pupils briefed on safety before taking part in activities
Accidental falls	All	Tables set out with clear access No obstructions on the floor	Check that all areas of the floor are clear No table cloths hanging down to the floor

Example of a risk assessment chart

Tips on how to complete your event assignments

Your introduction

Things to include when writing up your introduction:

- Always include the event outline at the start of your work. Your teacher may give you this as an introduction to the event.
- It's a good idea to outline keywords and explain what they mean.
- Plan how the work will be completed. Include deadlines and dates.
- Explain what you have been asked to do. You could include the people involved and a 'thought shower' to start your ideas rolling.

Research

Your research should give you answers to the following questions:

- What is the event?
- Where and when will it take place?
- What are the roles of the people in your group? (You might want to include job descriptions and examples where they are used in the hospitality and catering industry.)

What about a garden party?

- What resources and equipment will be required?
- What services are already available for your target customers?
- What do customers want? (If you are carrying out a questionnaire, remember to include questions about dietary requirements.)

Analyse all your research, looking carefully at whether it is necessary. Why is it included? What is the relevance of the piece of work in relation to the event?

Planning

Your planning should include:

- a detailed action plan. Who will do what in the event? Try to show a range of different skills over the two events. For example, if you do most of the cooking in the first event, do the serving in the second event. The more skills you show, the more you will achieve.
- risk assessment for the event, not just for the cooking! Remember to include fire procedures, health and safety of guests, wheelchair access.
- menus produced. If you have a menu, include a copy in your coursework.
- costing out and portion control. You should include information on how much the products cost to make and any profit included. You should also include evidence of portion control within the product. How many does it serve?

- how the event will look. You should add information on how you would like the area to be set out.
- trialling recipes. During the preparation for your event you will trial recipes and ideas. Include them in your work and remember to evaluate how they look and taste.

Carrying out the event

When you carry out the event you should:

- collect evidence for your portfolio of how you have carried out the event effectively
- show a range of practical skills across the **two** events
- include written and photographic evidence of the event
- include customer care. How will you make sure that customers are happy during the event?
- work hygienically and show safe working practices.

Photographs are good evidence to show you were dressed correctly, wearing a hat and apron. Always identify who you are in any group pictures.

Evaluation

You will need to evaluate all areas of the portfolio work, from the research and planning stage through to the event itself.

- Explain what worked well.
- Explain what you would change if you did it again, and why.
- Include any customer satisfaction comments or thank-you letters and explain what they are.
- Include any newspaper cuttings and give details about them.

Presentation of your work

Your work should be clearly presented with evidence of all areas of the event. If possible, word-process your work so that you can make alterations and include photographs in your work. You can also include spreadsheets for costing out the events.

Always present your work in a logical order with sub-headings, as this makes it easier for the examiner to moderate your work.

If you include photographs, make sure you have identified where you appear in them.

For group activities, it is fine to include evidence from other team members, so long as you annotate the work clearly, stating why you have included it.

For example, if someone is in charge of funding the event they may include a costing sheet, which they give to the rest of the group. You can include this, providing you state clearly that it is not your work but essential to the assignment as it shows the role of the financial advisor. You would in return give them your report of the role you took in the event.

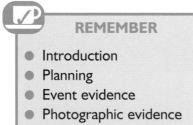

If you are doing GCSE Catering, you will be required to carry out practical assessments.

Choosing dishes and planning your practical tasks

Choosing dishes

Choosing the right dishes to make for a practical is one of the most difficult tasks. Try to include a variety of colours, textures and flavours.

Also, try to choose dishes that show skill, such as:

- rubbing-in e.g. pastry, crumble, biscuits
- creaming e.g. fairy cakes, pineapple upside-down pudding, piped biscuits
- whisking e.g. gateau
- sauce-making e.g. béchamel or custard
- yeast mixtures e.g. pizza or bread rolls
- dishes using high-risk foods like meat, chicken and fish e.g. chicken chasseur, lasagne.

Lasagne

Try also to make some dishes that show a variety of cooking methods, such as boiling, baking, frying, grilling. A careful choice of dishes means you will get off to a good start with your task.

Reasons for choice

Below is a list of factors that you may want to consider before making your choices. (Note: Not all of the reasons given here will apply to every assessment. Use only those that are relevant.)

1. Dishes show a variety of colours (state the colours of each dish – remember to avoid all cream, brown or green).
2. Dishes show a variety of textures (chewy, soft, crunchy, crisp, etc).
3. Cost – state if the dishes are economical, if you are using food in season, if you are using a wide or a basic range of commodities.

4. Time taken to prepare and cook. All dishes should 'fit' into the given time (consider setting time as well as cooking or cooling time).
5. Sale-able. Customers in a restaurant would be willing to pay. (Note: Do not use this reason for assessment where you are preparing food for people in a home or school meals.)
6. Easy to portion control and to serve. State how you will portion all dishes i.e. use of garnish or decoration, use of spoons, ladles, etc.
7. Dishes will look attractive (explain garnish/decoration to help the dishes 'stand out').
8. Dishes show a range of skill. You must include at least one high-level (hands-on) skill e.g. pastry, cake, biscuit, scone, bread, sauce mixture.
9. Dishes show a variety of cooking methods (bake, fry, grill, boil).
10. Dishes should be suitable for given groups (when preparing meals for children, vegetarian or old people) or given situations e.g. dinner, lunch, buffet party, afternoon tea, celebration meal.
11. Nutritive value – this is important when preparing meals for children or old people in homes who have little choice about what they eat. Nutritive value should be included for all dishes chosen.
12. Healthy eating – where possible, include dishes that are low in fat, sugar and salt and high in fibre i.e. include wholemeal products, cereals, fresh fruit and vegetables to show that you are aware of current thinking on nutrition.
13. All your dishes should be suitable for producing in bulk.
14. Can be refrigerated/frozen for use another time. Can be kept hot (above 63°C) or reheated safely. (Note: Reheated food should not be served to high-risk groups.)
15. Make reference to personal hygiene and critical control points – how you will prepare yourself, where you will take extra hygiene/safety precautions (e.g. preparation of chicken – keep refrigerated, handle as little as possible, cook thoroughly, wash equipment and hands thoroughly to prevent cross contamination).

A healthy dish: salmon with spring vegetables

Writing a time plan

When you have decided on your menu or choice of dishes, your next task is to write your time plan. Many students have found the following method helpful. Although it takes a lot of time to start with, it makes sure that you don't miss out any of the stages.

First, go through each dish and make a numbered list of all the stages in making each one, from mise-en-place through to serving.

An example is given below for the chosen menu.

> **MENU**
> Chicken chasseur
> Creamed potatoes
> Peas
> Strawberry gateau

Example stages for time plan

Chicken chasseur
1. Skin chicken, peel and chop vegetables.
2. Fry chicken. Remove from pan.
3. Fry onion and bacon, add flavour and the rest of the ingredients for sauce.
4. Re-add chicken and simmer on hob for 45 mins.
5. Place chicken in serving dish.
6. Garnish and serve.

Strawberry gateau
1. Make sponge base (whisk eggs and sugar till thick, fold in flour). Bake Gas 6/200°C for 15–20 mins.
2. Turn onto wire rack and allow to cool.
3. Whip cream and cut strawberries.
4. Decorate gateaux and refrigerate (portion control).
5. Serve.

Creamed potatoes
1. Peel and chop potatoes, cover with fresh cold water.
2. Salt – bring to boil.
3. Simmer for 20 mins.
4. Drain – mash with butter and milk.
5. Place in serving dish, level top and fork round.
6. Garnish and serve.

Peas
1. Place peas in boiling water.
2. Simmer for 7–10 mins.
3. Drain – add butter.
4. Serve.

You then need to 'dovetail' each stage of each dish to make a time plan, as shown in the example below. Start your plan with the dishes that need the longest cooking time, cooling time or setting time. Finish with the final garnish and serving. Allow at least 10 minutes for final garnish and decoration before serving. Make sure you start and finish tasks at the correct times.

Time plan

Time	Order of work	Special points
8.30	Mise-en-place. Set up table. Collect serving dishes. Peel and chop potatoes. Prepare garnishes and decorations (whip cream, fan strawberries). Chop parsley. Peel and chop onion, dice bacon, chop mushrooms. Tidy table for start.	Refrigerate perishables (chicken and cream). Light oven – Gas 6 or 200°C.
9.00	Gateau: Make sponge using whisking method. (Whisk eggs and sugar till thick, fold in flour.) Divide between two tins.	Fold in gently. Bake – 20 mins.
9.20	Chicken chasseur: Fry chicken to seal. Remove and place on plate. Fry bacon and onion, add flour, tomatoes, stock, puree etc. Re-add chicken pieces and mushrooms. Simmer.	Use tongs to turn chicken. Very low heat for at least 45 mins.
9.40	Check gateaux base – remove from oven if cooked. Turn onto wire rack.	Should feel 'springy' in centre.
9.45	Wash up. Put potatoes onto boil. When boiling, reduce the heat and simmer. Stir chasseur.	Add tsp salt. Simmer 20 mins on low heat.
9.55	Decorate gateau with swirls of cream and fanned strawberries.	Remember portion control. Refrigerate.
10.05	Wash up. Boil water in kettle for peas.	

10.10	Put peas in pan. Add boiling water. Simmer for 7–10 minutes.	Medium heat.
10.15	Check potatoes – if cooked drain and mash with butter and milk. Spread in dish. Fork round, garnish with sprig of parsley.	Cold water soak for pans. Place in oven to keep hot.
10.20	Drain peas. Place in serving dish. Place chasseur in serving dish and garnish with a row of parsley.	Wipe edges of dishes.
10.25	Take gateau from fridge. Place on table with main course dishes.	
10.30	Serve all dishes.	
	Complete washing up.	

Shopping list

The shopping list for your assessment must be written accurately in order to gain full marks. You must identify food correctly (e.g. caster sugar, **plain** flour, **block** margarine) and give the total amounts needed.

Use all metric quantities.

Using the following headings may help you identify the different commodities more easily:

- Butcher/Fishmonger.
- Grocer.
- Greengrocer.
- Dairy.

Under the heading of Greengrocer, group foods into vegetables, salad, fruit and fresh herbs.

> **REMEMBER**
>
> Remember to include all garnishes and decorations on your shopping list.

Equipment list

List the equipment you need to carry out your assessment under three headings:

1. Preparation.
2. Special equipment.
3. Serving dishes.

Heading 1 (Preparation) should contain all the equipment you need to make and cook your dishes, including bowls, knives, piping bags, baking trays etc.

Heading 2 (Special equipment) should list any special equipment you need (especially as it is limited in some rooms) e.g. microwave, toaster, hand-held mixer.

Heading 3 (Serving dishes) should list all the serving dishes, flats, vegetable dishes and cake stands that you need. Also include here any paper doilies and dish papers.

You should not have to use more than one or two items of the same type (e.g. mixing bowls). If you do this you will have too much washing up, and (more important) you will lose marks!

Evaluation

Use the following questions to help you carry out your evaluation.

1. Do you think that you have answered the task correctly? What dishes did you make? Why were the dishes suitable?
2. Did you include a variety of cooking skills (e.g. sauce making, pastry making, bread making, rubbing in, creaming, whisking)? State what skills you used for each dish.
3. Did you include a variety of cooking methods (e.g. boiling, baking, toasting, frying, poaching, microwaving)? State what methods you used for each dish.
4. Did you plan the order of work successfully i.e. did you make the dishes in the correct order so that the food was hot, cold or set as required? If not – how could you change your plan? Did you manage your time well?
5. How well did you work throughout? Was your mise-en-place successful? If so, why and if not, why not? Did you work to time? Were you able to control the hob and oven? Did you handle mixtures successfully (especially pastry, cake and sauces)? Did you follow the hygiene and safety rules throughout the test time? Justify your comments.
6. Did your completed dishes turn out as you expected or hoped? Make comments about the colour and flavour of the food (you must taste it!), the number of portions, portion size, use of the correct-sized dishes for the amounts of food, attractive garnish or decoration, whether or not food was hot, cold or set as needed. What about the effect of the 'whole' table? Did your food look good enough to eat?
7. Finally, suggest any improvements you would make if you were given the same task to do again. If you would choose different dish(es), say what you would choose

and why. If you could improve the 'making' say how and why. If you would improve the presentation or change the order of work, suggest how and why.

Costings

If you are asked to work out the cost of your dishes you must set it out as discussed in lessons (i.e. with each recipe written out as a list on the left-hand side of the page with the costing on the right-hand side). Use shop receipts where possible.

1. Calculate the total cost of each dish.
2. Divide each dish by the number of portions to give cost per portion.
3. Calculate an approximate selling price of each portion by multiplying by at least three or four times the cost. Make sure you have rounded up to the nearest 10p. (Note: The selling price needs to include food costs, labour, overheads and profit, so it must be at least three times the cost).

Make a comment on whether you think your food would be considered good value for money if sold to paying customers in a restaurant.

REMEMBER

Don't use the word 'nice' in your evaluation – it's too general. Try to find words that describe the food and your work more clearly.

WORK-RELATED EXPERIENCE

If you choose to participate in work-related experience for Unit 3 you will need to complete an in-depth review of your work placement. Your placement should last long enough for you to get a good overview of the establishment.

What you need to cover

You will need to include information on the following areas:

- promotion and sales
- working within the industry – personal and professional skills
- the journey of food from supplier to customer
- dress code
- equipment – range and use
- standards of service
- customer care
- HACCP and risk assessment.

Before you start your work experience get in touch with your contact at the establishment and let them know that you have to complete your coursework while on placement. Ask your teacher for a copy of the specification requirements and a covering letter to take with you. When you get there, talk to your contact, and explain what you need to find out.

KEY WORDS

Promotion: advertising your business to get more trade.
Skills: the abilities you have to complete the job.
Policies: rules that are in place to enable a safe working environment.
Customer care: how well you look after paying guests.

REMEMBER

Remember, the hospitality and catering industry is very busy, so choose an appropriate time to ask for help. Don't ask in the middle of service!

Your folder will be assessed on five areas. They are

- local provision
- in-depth investigation
- policies and procedures
- your work-related experience
- evaluation.

Let's look at each key issue in detail. This will help you decide what you need to find out and how to record your information.

Promotion and sales

You could include this information in your introduction. When you know where you are going on placement, you can investigate how they promote the business. For example, do they advertise online, in newspapers, with flyers or by word of mouth? You can find out this information before you go by making a pre-placement visit or investigating online.

ACTIVITY

Try to find out answers to the following questions:

- What facilities do they have?
- Who is the target market? (customers)
- Are they busy all year?
- Do they hold special events like weddings and conferences?
- How do they promote their facilities (TV, radio, flyers, vouchers etc)?
- How many similar businesses are in the area?
- What is the competition like?

You should understand why the establishment needs to promote the business and how it can bring in more customers. Think about the time of year and relevant events – for example, more weddings take place in spring and summer than any other time of year. So some hotels may hold a wedding fayre to promote their business and to show prospective customers what is on offer. They could also invite local businesses (such as photographers, wedding clothes and wedding cake companies) to attend, for a small fee. This helps to promote the business and also brings in money.

Once you have gathered this information you can record it as an introduction to your coursework. It shows what you expect the place to be like when you are on placement.

ACTIVITY

Find the following words in the grid:

customer, activity, hotel, wedding, business, radio, flyers, TV, event, menu, promote, busy, sales, bill.

c	s	y	t	i	v	i	t	c	a
g	u	r	e	t	o	m	o	r	p
n	s	s	e	n	i	s	u	b	a
i	e	r	t	y	m	e	n	u	s
d	v	a	c	o	l	l	h	a	y
d	e	d	t	v	m	f	l	p	s
e	n	i	h	o	t	e	l	i	u
w	t	o	g	h	s	r	r	s	b

Working within the industry

In this section you should identify various jobs within the hospitality and catering industry and how they link together to form an efficient service for customers.

> ### ACTIVITY
> When you arrive on placement, make a list of all the jobs available within the establishment. Then interview members of staff to find out answers to the following questions:
>
> - What qualifications do you need?
> - How long is the training for the job?
> - Where can you complete your training – in-house or college?
> - What are the chances of promotion within the job?
> - What are the skills required to do the job?
> - How long has the person been doing the job?
> - What previous experience have they got in the industry?

It is a good idea to interview more than one person – then you can compare the results. This will help you when you are writing up your information. You could then ask yourself if you would be able to do the job yourself. What additional skills do you need to acquire to enable you to complete the job? You might learn some of these skills while you are on placement, or when you get back to school or college.

When you have gathered all your information, you will need to write it up clearly and add it to your portfolio of evidence. If you have been given any documents or information that you would like to include, you must annotate it clearly and state why you are including it in your work.

QUALIFICATIONS IN THE HOSPITALITY AND CATERING INDUSTRY:

GCSE
NVQ levels 1, 2, 3
City and Guilds. 706/1 706/2 707
National Diplomas

Remember to include information about the work you complete while on placement. This should not be just a diary! Take account of what you are learning, what new skills you have acquired and what you have found out while doing the job. You could include an account of something that has happened to you or to someone else, and analyse your feelings about that event.

Once again, include photographs. Always ask for permission before you take them. If you include photos you must annotate them clearly and show who you are.

The journey of food from supplier to customer

You should be able to identify what steps are involved in the preparation of food. You must find out about the various types of foods used and their origin.

> **ACTIVITY**
> While on your work placment, try to find out answers to the following questions:
>
> - What foods are bought from local farmers and traders?
> - What foods are bought from within the region?
> - Are some foods bought from abroad? If so, why?
> - Does the company use organic foods or fair trade foods?
> - How are foods ordered and how often?

The next area to include is food storage. You should include information on how and when the food is delivered, as well as the procedures used to take and check deliveries.

> **ACTIVITY**
> Find out about:
>
> - stock rotation
> - safe food storage
> - checking food products on arrival
> - temperatures of foods delivered
> - use of refrigerators, freezers and ambient storage.

You will also need to include information on kitchen production, presentation of food and types of service.

> **ACTIVITY**
> - Look at the different types of service within the industry.
> - Does the establishment cook to order, batch produce?
> - Find out about the types of service they provide.
> - What are the advantages of that type of service to the establishment?

> **ACTIVITY**
> Find the following words in the grid:
>
> organic, plate, local, customer, produce, supply, service, batch, buffet, order, cook, checks, store.

l	o	c	a	l	d	h	t	s	c
s	y	o	j	h	c	o	e	c	u
k	l	o	l	t	e	r	f	i	s
c	p	k	a	r	v	d	f	n	t
e	p	b	o	i	e	e	u	a	o
h	u	t	c	s	o	r	b	g	m
c	s	e	e	t	a	l	p	r	e
p	r	o	d	u	c	e	p	o	r

Dress code

In this section you should identify the need for specialist clothing within the establishment. You will need to find

out why dress code changes for different staff within the different areas.

Some companies have a specific dress code for their staff. The colours may be the same, but the uniform may be different for staff in different areas. For example, wait staff may wear black trousers with a corporate colour top, and a white apron. Staff in the bar may wear the same uniform but with a black apron. Staff on reception may wear a suit with the same colour top. This will help staff and customers differentiate between the two departments.

Some staff wear specialist clothing for their job. Chefs have to wear 'whites', strong safe shoes, apron and hat. This not only protects them but also protects the food as the uniform is clean. The clothing worn by a chef is durable, easily washed and practical for the job they do. Strong shoes are important to protect from spills and damage.

It is important for reception staff to look smart as they are the first members of staff seen by the customers. Most staff wear badges that carry the company name and logo as well as their own name. This shows they are part of the corporate company.

One corporate company you will know is McDonald's. Staff are identified by the uniform they wear. Some staff wear a shirt that is a different colour from the shirts worn by the majority of workers. This often shows that they are more experienced.

ACTIVITY

● Find a picture of a food worker wearing protective clothing. Label the picture and state why the clothing is being worn.
● Find out about corporate uniforms used in the hotel industry and in fast-food chains like McDonalds.
● What are the advantages of having a uniform provided by the company you work for?

Equipment – range and use

This section is all about the safe use of equipment in the industry. You should be able to identify a range of specialist equipment and explain how to use it safely and hygienically.

You should look at a range of equipment including:

● hand equipment
● powered equipment

KEY WORDS

Protective: shielding, making safe.
Industry: business or trade.
Corporate: the group or chain of businesses. Can be shared, as in uniform or identity.
Identify: recognise, discover.
Wait staff: waiters and waitresses.

- food storage
- kitchen area
- restaurant area.

Hand equipment

This could include electric mixers and blenders in the kitchen area. It could also include hand-held credit-card payment facilities used in the restaurant area. Another area to look at is housekeeping. Try to list hand equipment used in this area. All electrical equipment must be checked for safety every year.

Powered equipment

A large range of powered equipment is used in the industry. Coffee machines, toasters, hot and cold service counters are often used in the restaurant area. Large-scale mixers, microwaves, ovens, hot plates and grills are used in the kitchens. Computers are used across all areas. Industrial cleaners are used in the guest rooms, food service areas and kitchens. EPOS (electronic point of sale) can be used to send orders from the restaurant and bar to the kitchen and reception, this assists staff with customers' bills.

Food storage

Large-scale refrigerators and freezers are used. Some larger establishments may use walk-in food storage. It is important to check the temperatures of these regularly and to keep a record of the results.

> **ACTIVITY**
> - Find out how EPOS works.
> - Identify three pieces of industrial machinery used in the kitchen area.
> - Describe how to use each one safely.
> - Find out how often the food storage temperatures are taken.
> - What temperature should the following be: freezer, refrigerator, dry store?

Standards of service

It is important that you understand about standards of service and how to make sure that staff are providing reliable services to customers.

You should be able to identify acceptable service standards in the following working areas:

● reception, front-of-house, food service
● meeting, greeting and bidding farewell
● responding to enquiries
● dealing with complaints
● presenting bills.

Customers like to feel welcome and important when they visit any establishment. The first members of staff they encounter are reception or front-of-house, so it is important that the staff are friendly and approachable. If there is a queue, try to acknowledge that you are aware that people are waiting and tell them you won't be long. When you are able to deal with the customer, apologise for the wait. When customers leave, say 'thank you' and 'goodbye'. Remember that 'manners are free' and they go a long way to making the customer happy and satisfied with the service they have received.

> **ACTIVITY**
> Try to find out:
>
> ● how customers are greeted at reception
> ● how complaints are handled
> ● how customers are approached for their orders in the restaurant and bar
> ● if staff are friendly and helpful
> ● the 'extras' that are provided with the coffee in conference rooms.
>
> When you are recording your information, try to include an incident that happened on your placement. Describe how it was dealt with and how the customer felt afterwards. Do you think the incident was dealt with correctly? What would you have done?

KEY WORDS

Complaint: expression of dissatisfaction.
Response: how you react verbally and in your body language.
Review: look back on something to see how it was dealt with.

Standards of service link with customer care, the next area we look at. Customer care is a major aspect of the industry. Most establishments have standards that must be met by all staff. Reviews and training take place regularly.

Customer care

In this section of your work you should include information on the importance of good customer care. You should be able to identify, apply and evaluate customer care effectively. Customer care is not just about talking to the customers when there is a problem. The following also need to be considered:

- attitude
- appearance
- manner
- body language
- voice.

We have all seen or heard about incidents of poor customer care. Perhaps you have been on the receiving end yourself. Let's look at a scenario of events. See how many things you identify as good and poor customer care.

Bob and Sue have pre-booked a hotel close to an event they are going to see on a Sunday. They set off to the hotel on the Saturday afternoon. Half way there, they receive a call from the hotel stating that there is a problem with the room. The hotel staff tell Bob and Sue that they have arranged for them to stay in another hotel close to the event. Bob and Sue feel that this is acceptable and thank the hotel for letting them know.

They arrive at the new hotel at around 4 pm. On arrival they explain to the staff what has happened. The receptionist tells them the other hotel had double booked, as the event was so popular. Bob is a little annoyed about this, but does not say anything. He then asks what time they could have their evening meal. He is told to ask the manager, who is near the bar. The manager says they are very busy with a carvery buffet at six, but they can eat around half past six. Bob thanks the manager and goes to find the room.

At half past six, Bob and Sue make their way to the dining room. It is very busy, so they check it is still alright to eat there. The manager tells them to take a seat and that someone will be with them shortly. At half past seven, they are still waiting for their order to be taken. The group having the carvery are still being served and another group are waiting to come in. Bob goes to speak to the manager again. He is told that someone will be along to take their order and the manager apologises for the inconvenience. At eight they are still waiting, so Sue goes to speak to the manager. The manager says he is very sorry but they have two carvery buffets booked and it is the first time they have done an event like this. He sends one of the waitresses to take their order straight away and offers them a free bottle of wine. They eventually get their meal at nine o clock, at no charge.

ACTIVITY

There are examples of both good and bad customer care in this scenario. Identify these as a group and discuss what you think should have happened.

When you are thinking about customer care, you should also take into account the way in which the staff respond to the customer. It is important to show good manners toward the customer. Your appearance also goes a long way, as does your body language.

If a customer has a complaint you should:

● apologise
● tell them you will deal with the complaint
● take their name and room number or address
● pass on the information to your supervisor or manager
● go back and let the customer know it is being dealt with.

REMEMBER

Remember that your supervisor or manager will notice your appearance and body language. It will not look good if you respond to the customer by saying, 'Yeah, so what do you want me to do about it?' while slouching with your hands in your pockets and chewing gum.

The supervisor or manager should then:

● find out the details
● speak to the member of staff concerned
● explain to the customer what has happened
● offer some form of compensation
● apologise to the customer again
● offer additional training to the staff on customer care.

ACTIVITY

Role-play:

- In small groups, think about something that a customer might complain about.
- Act out the event, showing poor customer care.
- Discuss the role-play with the rest of the class.
- Act out the role-play again, this time showing good customer care.
- Record your thoughts in your book.

> **KEY WORDS**
>
> Attitude: The way in which you approach customers.
> Appearance: The way you look to customers. It is important to look clean and smart.
> Manner: The way you speak to customers.
> Body language: The way in which your body reflects your mood.
> Voice: The tone of voice you use to customers.

Policies and procedures

You will be expected to identify one or more policies used within the placement and to demonstrate that you understand how to apply these within the hospitality and catering industry. It is important to annotate the policies in your portfolio, not just to put them in without an explanation.

You may want to look again at the section on HACCP in Unit 1.

Examples of policies you may be given:

- HACCP (Hazard Analysis and Critical Control Points).
- Risk assessment.
- Personal hygiene and safety including training.
- Fire procedures/first aid.
- Customer care.
- Reporting accidents.
- Standards of service.
- Environmental issues.

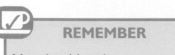

You do not have to include all of these in your portfolio, but if you include them you must remember to annotate them fully.

It is a good idea to identify one of the policies that you have used while on your placement. One of the first things you will have been shown is what to do in the event of a fire. You may have been given a copy of the fire procedure.

ACTIVITY
Explain why it is important that everyone knows what to do in the event of a fire and how this affects the customers.

You may decide to include how HACCP is used in the industry and to give examples that you have seen while on placement. For example, in the kitchen, explain how the food is prepared and cooked to a high standard of safety. Or in the restaurant, how food is kept to the correct temperature and served, avoiding cross-contamination.

You may have seen an accident and could give a detailed account of how it was dealt with. Were the company procedures followed correctly? If any cleaning has taken place in public areas, what procedures did the company take to ensure customer safety?

Your evaluation

This is the final section of your portfolio. In this section, you should look back at each area of your work and state what you have found out.

You will need to include:

- how the establishment meets the needs of its customers

- your own experience working as a team member

- the skills and knowledge you have acquired while on placement.

Your evaluation should be detailed and reflect all areas of your work, including how well you think you have done in all areas of your work.

ACTIVITY

Ask yourself the following questions:

- How did you feel before you went on your placement, and how do you feel about it now?
- What new skills have you learned?
- What skills do you still need if you want to enter the hospitality and catering industry?
- How did you work as a team member?
- How does team work affect the day-to-day running of the establishment?
- What have you found out about company policies and procedures?
- How are policies used in the industry!
- What area did you enjoy working in the most?
- How easy or difficult was it to find out all the information you required?
- Did you keep your portfolio up to date or did you leave it all till the end?

How well do you think you know the industry now?

ACTIVITY

Before you hand in your portfolio, check back and make sure it is all in order.

- Have you annotated pictures and policies clearly?
- Is your work clearly presented?
- Have you included information on each of the key issues?
- Does it show evidence of your role while on placement?
- Have you included your evaluation?

Well done!

Example question

In this section we look at an example question and show how you would go about tackling this part of your assessment.

The question given below is an example of the type you will get.

> **THE QUESTION**
>
> Investigate and compare **two** catering outlets in your local area. You could choose hotels, fast-food outlets, fish and chip shops, kebab houses, take-away outlets, restaurants or cafeterias.

How to tackle the question

You should aim to compare two similar types of outlets e.g. McDonald's and Burger King, Pizza Hut and Pizza Express, Harvester and Beefeater. Choosing two very different outlets will not give you an effective comparison.

The sections given below show how to tackle the question step by step. You should use a similar approach for the question you are given.

Introduction

You will need to include a well-presented paragraph at the beginning that clearly states the aims of your project (in this case, what outlets you intend to investigate and why).

Plan of action

This could be a flow-chart or spider diagram that gives details of your plan. You need to include a clear explanation of how you will collect the information you need and how you will set out your study.

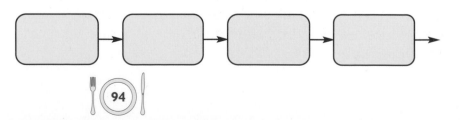

Area of study

For this question, you should be comparing factors like the ones in the following list. Read through the list, then choose four areas to compare. (These are just examples. You may think of other areas that you could compare in the two outlets.)

1. Promotion and sales – types of promotional activity (how and where the outlets advertise, and who their advertisements are aimed at i.e. the target market or potential customers).
2. Uniform of staff/dress code (e.g. is it appropriate for the tasks that are being done?)
3. Standard of food – menu on offer, prices, special meal deals (e.g. for children or the elderly, party plans, meals suitable for vegetarians).
4. Standard of service and customer care.
5. Health, safety and hygiene of premises – include kitchen areas, dining areas, reception areas, accommodation areas and toilet facilities (as appropriate).
6. The use of packaging for take-away food.
7. Facilities for people with disabilities.

Note: You must remember to compare 'like for like'. For example, you can't choose to look at the staff uniform and menu that is on offer in one outlet, and then at the toilet facilities and standard of customer care in the other!

Background research/report/information

This could be in the form of reports on your visits, print-outs from the internet (but no more than one or two of these), and other information you have collected during your visits, such as menus, packaging, leaflets etc.

You should put your diagrams and photographs of layouts, and your annotated photographs of the outside and inside of the outlets into this section.

Primary research

This is usually done in the form of a questionnaire or survey. You need to show that you have investigated your chosen outlets and collected customer and/or staff comments. Use ICT to prepare graphs of your questionnaire results where possible.

Using diagrams, illustrations, photos and graphs

You need to make sure that any graphs you include are accurate graphs and that any photographs or diagrams you use are clear and relevant. Try to use a range of graphs and charts e.g. bar charts, pie diagrams, pictograms, star diagrams.

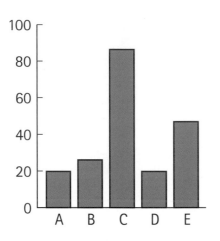

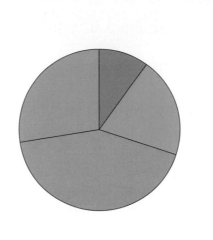

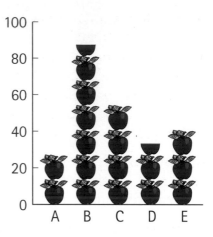

Conclusion

In the final section you should discuss and analyse all your results. What have you found out? Are the results as you expected, or do you find them surprising? You should comment on your findings.

You will need to discuss the results from all of the questions in your questionnaire or survey in order to achieve full marks. If you have compared the two outlets well, this will be quite straightforward.

Read the box below to see the kinds of points you should be making when you write up your findings.

REMEMBER

When you carry out your research, remember to ask ten or twenty people, so that it is easy to calculate percentages when you come to do your analysis.

EXAMPLE FINDINGS

'You will see from the answers to Question 1 that 80 per cent of the people I asked visit McDonald's at least once a week, but only 20 per cent visit Burger King at least once a week. I was not surprised by this result because there are two popular McDonald's outlets in the town and people of my age group prefer to visit McDonald's.'

'In Question 2 I asked people to rate the staff in the two outlets. Fifty per cent of the people I asked rated the staff in McDonald's as friendly and efficient, but 70 per cent of the people rated the staff in Burger King as friendly and efficient. I would agree with these findings. The staff in Burger King are more mature and treat all their customers well, whereas the staff in McDonald's are often young and sometimes a little 'offhand' when serving teenagers. Food is generally served more quickly in Burger King.'

So, to sum up, in your conclusion you need to:

- give the results of each of your questions **in words** (not just in numbers).
- say if you agree with your findings (and why).
- say if you disagree with your findings (and why).
- try to explain why you think you got a particular result (e.g. you may have carried out your survey with a limited age group).

At the end of your conclusion, suggest improvements for each of the outlets based on your findings.

Here are two improvements that were suggested in this case:

'If McDonald's made sure their young staff were trained more effectively they could provide a faster service.'

'Burger King needs to have disabled facilities on the ground floor in order to meet all customer needs.'

Evaluation and review

This needs to be written in four sections:

- Planning
- Methodology
- Results obtained
- Review.

Planning

Discuss the strengths or problems of the planning of your project.

Here is an example showing how to present your 'Planning' section:

'I was set the project in [*state when*], which meant I had time to plan the work effectively. I chose to compare two local outlets so that if I did forget anything I could visit again for more information/photos/ask more questions etc. I planned my questionnaire in sections, and made sure that I planned my visits carefully so that I collected everything I needed.'

Methodology

The example below shows how you could present your 'Methodology section:

'For my project I decided to compare layouts, menu, disabled facilities and the attitude of the staff. I collected the data at xx on xx [*state when and where you did this*] making sure that I visited both outlets at similar times for a fair comparison. I took photographs [*say whether or not they were successful, how you have used them, what others could you have taken*], collected leaflets, packaging etc [*say whether or not they were useful, comment on how they helped you complete your project*], devised and asked my questionnaire [*say how you did this — list of questions face-to-face/paper questionnaires for people to complete, who you asked, why this was valid.*]'

State if you collected all the data you needed (and say why, or why not). Comment on the 'fairness' of your data. How could you improve the method of collecting data for your project?

Results obtained

This should repeat the information in the results section of your conclusion, and comment on it.

Here is an example of how to present your 'Results obtained'.

'As you will see from my conclusion, McDonald's was rated higher than Burger King in terms of value for money, staff attitude etc, but was rated lower than Burger King in terms of menu choice and disabled facilities.

● My results show …
● Overall I was surprised that …
● I have found out /learned that …'

Review

What are the strengths and weaknesses of your project? You may feel you could have done better with some parts of your work.

For example:

● the planning – could you have started the project earlier, or planned more thoroughly?
● the methods used to obtain information – could you have asked more questions, given questionnaires to a wider range of people to obtain more valid results etc?
● the presentation – could you have made better use of ICT, included more photographs or more graphs etc?

Add brief notes to complete the following:

● If I did this project again I would change …
● If I did this project again I would improve …

Presentation

REMEMBER

Remember that marks are awarded for neat, clear, methodical work and using ICT where appropriate. Your project should look professional.

UNIT 4

THE ROLE OF THE HOSPITALITY AND CATERING INDUSTRY

You should know about the hospitality and catering industry in relation to:

- its role as a national employment provider
- the benefits to local communities
- the importance of links between hospitality and leisure, travel and tourism.

About the industry

The hospitality and catering industry is the biggest growing industry in the UK. There are over 250,000 people employed in the industry in the UK. About forty per cent of these are from the UK, the rest are from other countries. There is a great shortage of staff in the industry so some jobs are advertised abroad.

The hospitality and catering industry has links with tourism. People travel for work or pleasure and require food, drink and sometimes accommodation. Overseas visitors spend one-third of the cost of their holiday on accommodation and catering. Tourists also visit attractions such as fun fairs, historic buildings, art galleries, scenic views and special events. During these visits, catering and accommodation may be in great demand. However, the number of tourists tends to drop if the weather is bad.

The main organisations

There are several organisations involved in the industry. These are:

- HCIMA – Hotel and Catering International Management Association (now known as Institute of Hospitality)
- RIPH – Royal Institute of Public Health
- CIEH – Chartered Institute of Environmental Health
- SSC – Sector Skills Council
- People 1st – Sector skills council for hospitality, leisure and travel and tourism.
- BHA – British Hospitality Association
- BII – British Institute of Inn-Keeping
- RSPH – Royal Society for the Promotion of Health.

These associations help the industry meet the standards set to ensure all customers and staff are safe and staff are supported in their job.

> **ACTIVITY**
> Look at the organisations above and decide which ones are linked to food safety and hygiene.
>
> Which ones are linked to standards of service?
>
> Which ones are linked to staffing?

Corporate identity

Some companies within the hospitality and catering industry have their own corporate image, e.g. Forté Hotels and fast food outlets such as McDonald's.

They are easily identifiable by;

- the logo
- the uniform/dress code
- the menu
- the layout of the establishment.

Logo

Logos are used to encourage customers to recognise the establishment as they know what to expect from the company. They are used across all establishments within the company.

Uniform/dress code

Some companies insist all staff wear the same uniform; this makes them easily identifiable for staff and customers. It saves staff paying for uniforms and they are often cleaned by the company. The uniform may change depending on which area of the establishment they work in.

Menu

Often, the menu chosen in large companies is the same no matter where you are in the country or abroad, e.g. McDonald's, Brewer's Fayre or Beefeater. This enables the companies to arrange large orders with manufacturers and possibly to make big savings and therefore more profit. Customers get to know the menu and are familiar with it.

Layout

The layout of the establishment can be the same or similar across the country, this makes the customers feel secure and at home no matter where they are, e.g. Little Chef, McDonald's and Burger King. Again the customer knows what to expect in each of these.

Before starting to plan any menu, there are four basic questions that you should ask:

1. Who is going to eat the meal? Consider age, gender, occupation, specific dietary needs, etc.
2. When is it going to be eaten? Consider time of year, time of day, etc.
3. Where is it going to be eaten? Consider venue, space available, cooking or re-heating facilities available, etc.
4. What is going to be eaten? Consider time of day, type of menu requested e.g. sit down meal or buffet, special occasions, etc.

When these basic questions have been answered, there are many other factors to consider in planning a well-balanced menu. We look at the most important factor first – the nutritional needs of the customer.

Nutritional needs

Good health relies on good nutritious food. Nutritional needs must be considered carefully in residential establishments (such as care homes, hospitals, prisons, schools) where people have little choice about what they eat.

Everyone needs the following:

● protein – for growth and repair of body cells
● carbohydrates (starches and sugars) for energy and physical activity
● fats – for body warmth, energy and protection of body organs (e.g. the kidneys)
● vitamins and minerals – for protection against disease and to regulate body functions
● water – for body processes like digestion and for controlling body temperature
● fibre – for the healthy working of the digestive system.

The amount of each nutrient needed depends on a person's age, gender, occupation and lifestyle.

Young children

Young children need protein for growth and development. Children should be given small, attractive portions of food. They should be introduced to new foods gradually. Fatty foods and sugary foods and drinks should be avoided.

Teenagers

Teenagers also need a good supply of protein. Worries about being overweight and poor skin are typical of this age group. Eating five portions a day of fruit and vegetables will encourage healthy skin. Fruit and vegetables are high in vitamins and fibre and contain virtually no fat, so can help maintain a healthy weight. A good supply of iron is needed, especially for teenage girls when they start menstruation (periods). Again, fatty foods and sugary foods and drinks should be avoided. Careful and sensible eating is essential to lay down good habits for adulthood.

Pensioners

Pensioners need protein to repair worn out body cells. They need a good supply of calcium and Vitamin D in order to maintain healthy bones and teeth and iron to keep blood healthy. In winter time, they may need a little more fat in their diet to provide body warmth. Fresh fruit and vegetables are important for a good supply of vitamins and minerals. Old people may have digestive problems (an inability to digest certain foods) or may have difficulty cutting food (because of arthritis) or chewing food (because of false teeth).

Special diets

This aspect applies particularly to caterers who are planning meals for patients in hospitals or homes. In a hospital, dieticians will ensure the correct foods are given in the correct quantity. Generally foods rich in Vitamin C are given to help the healing process. Foods high in starch, sugar and fat are reduced so that patients do not put on too much weight. Foods are served in small, colourful portions to encourage eating if there is loss of appetite.

Other factors

Next, we look at other factors that you need to take into account when planning menus that are suitable for customers.

Vegetarian dishes

Vegetarian dishes are popular, especially when there are concerns about diseases and outbreaks of food poisoning linked to meat (salmonella, E-Coli, BSE ('mad cow' disease), 'bird flu', etc.) Vegetable dishes and salads help to satisfy customers and offer variety in terms of colour, texture and taste. They also make the menu cheaper to produce. See also page 112.

Religious and ethnic diets

People of some faiths do not eat meat. As a general rule, Jews and Muslims do not eat pork and Hindus do not eat beef. Most religious diets are catered for with either vegan or vegetarian dishes. By law, every restaurant must offer at least one dish that is suitable for vegetarians. In practice, most restaurants offer more than this, in order to attract customers. There are many 'ethnic' restaurants in the UK, each serving a mix of traditional and 'anglicised' dishes (for example, Indian, Chinese and Thai dishes are all very popular).

Time of year and weather

Generally, we prefer hot food in cold weather and cold food in hot weather. In winter, dishes such as stews, casseroles and roasts are in demand. In summer, salads and foods like fish and chicken in light sauces are preferred. Caterers often make use of foods 'in season' when they are cheap and good quality to create popular seasonal menus. Traditionally, special dishes are served at certain times of the year, for example roast turkey or goose at Christmas, pancakes on Shrove Tuesday, Spring lamb at Easter. Muslims traditionally eat roast lamb at Tobaski or Eid.

Type of customer

Customers choose where and what to eat because of many different reasons. They may want a celebration meal, a snack while they are out shopping, a lunch to socialise with friends, a meal during a business meeting or a buffet party to celebrate a christening, wedding or birthday. Customers will have different needs at different times.

Time available

As a general rule, the shorter the time available to cook, serve and eat the food, the more limited (smaller) the menu. Fast-food outlets offer a limited menu, where all items can be cooked quickly. Customers queue and collect their own food, pay before they eat, and find their own tables or take food away. If they eat on site, they are encouraged to clear their own tables at the end.

Restaurants such as Harvester and Beefeater offer customers a more relaxed 'meal experience'. Customers wait to be seated and they order drinks and meals from serving staff. They collect their own salads from the salad cart, but meals and drinks are served to them. The tables are cleared and the bill is taken to the customer after they have eaten. Generally, self service is much faster than waiter/waitress service.

Price of menu

STARTERS	
Tomato and basil soup	£3.75
Melon and Parma ham	£3.75
Breaded prawns with sweet chilli dipping sauce	£4.99
Garlic bread	£3.50

Customers are generally willing to pay a fair price for a fair portion. The price the caterer can charge will depend on the quality of the food and the surroundings. The price you would expect to pay for a meal in McDonald's would not be the same as you would expect to pay in a five-star hotel, where you are paying not only for the food but the service and the surroundings.

Caterers working in residential establishments like hospitals, homes, prisons and schools usually have only a limited budget, so have to keep costs to a minimum.

Commercial establishments have to make a profit in order to stay in business. The selling price (price shown on the menu) must consider:

● food costs
● overheads (gas, electricity, lighting, rates and rent)
● labour costs (staff wages)
● profit.

The actual food costs are calculated at about forty per cent of the selling price. This means that if a dish costs £4 per portion to make, it would be sold for £10 per portion.

Portion control

Portion control concerns the amount of each menu item produced and served. It will depend upon the type of customer, the actual food item (some foods are very rich and only served in small portions) and the selling price of the food.

Good portion control is needed to:

Apple crumble made in individual portions

- keep costs down
- keep losses in food preparation and serving to a minimum
- to offer customers a 'satisfying' portion without waste
- to make a profit.

Portions can be 'marked' in the kitchen i.e. cutting lines are marked on dishes to show how big the portions should be. Careful garnishes or decorations (e.g. on a gateau or cheesecake) will also indicate portion size. There is also a range of equipment that can be used to portion food:

- scoops – used for ice cream, mashed potatoes
- ladles – used for soups, sauces and gravies
- fruit juice glasses – for fruit juice
- individual pie dishes – shepherds pie, fish pie, steak and onion pie, steak and kidney pie, lasagne
- ramekins – egg custards, mousses, pâtés
- sundae dishes – fruit salads
- individual moulds – jellies, mousses
- individual pudding basins – summer pudding, Christmas pudding, steamed pudding, sticky toffee pudding
- coupés – ice cream
- butter-pat machines – butter
- milk dispensers – milk
- soup plates or bowls
- serving spoons /tablespoons – fruit or vegetables.

Ability of chef/cook

The ability of the cook has a great influence on the menu offered. If staff are not highly trained it would be better to offer a simple menu that can be beautifully cooked and served. Many establishments rely on cook-chill or cook-freeze dishes. These need 'regeneration' (heating to required temperature) only and therefore do not need skilled staff. The more convenience foods used, the lower the level of skill needed.

A combi oven

An industrial steamer

A deep fat fryer

Equipment available

The amount of equipment will depend on how complicated the menu is, the type of food to be cooked and the number of meals to be served. Some foods (for example cook-chill foods) only need regeneration so there is no need for a full range of kitchen equipment. If fresh foods are used a full range of preparation and cooking equipment is needed.

Methods of cooking

A menu will be more attractive to customers if food is cooked in a variety of ways (e.g. boiled, baked, fried, grilled, poached, roasted, stewed). In a small or busy kitchen it is important to consider the cooking methods carefully, otherwise some pieces of equipment will be in constant use and cause delays, while other pieces of equipment may not be used at all. For example, if a lot of fried food is on offer, the friture (deep-fat fryer) may be over-used. Also, too much fried food on a menu will not offer customers a healthier option.

Here are two examples of poor menu planning:

- fried fish and chips followed by apple fritters (all fried)
- Irish stew, boiled potatoes and peas followed by stewed rhubarb and custard (all cooked in liquid).

Ability of serving staff

Many high-class establishments (e.g. five-star hotels) used to have highly trained wait staff who were able to provide silver service i.e. transfer food from a serving dish to the customers plate with great skill. Nowadays, the majority of high-class establishments use 'plated service' where the food is styled in the kitchen by the chef and served direct to the customer. The ability to look after customers and provide good customer care is considered to be more important than service skills.

Balance

To achieve a good balance, choose courses that vary from light to heavy. That way, customers will not feel bloated, nor will they think that they have not had their money's worth.

Balance means considering all of the following things.

Variety of ingredients

Try not to repeat ingredients from one course to another e.g. tomato soup followed by mixed grill served with chipped potatoes, tomatoes and peas.

Colour

Add colourful vegetables, salads, garnishes or decorations if possible to 'lift' the colour of food on the plate. Remember that white, cream, green and brown are 'dead' colours and too much of one of these colours will make food look boring and flat.

Flavour

Do not repeat strong flavours from one course to another e.g. garlic mushrooms followed by lasagne and garlic bread. Use strong-flavoured foods and herbs with care. Try not to over-season food so that customers cannot taste the natural flavours.

Texture

Contrasting textures are important to give variety and interest to a meal e.g. croutons with soup, wafers with ice-cream. Try to include foods that are soft and foods that need to be chewed, bitten or crunched. Remember that cooking changes the texture of food, so cooking times are important when cooking foods like rice, pasta, vegetables and steaks.

Shape

This is particularly important when serving buffet food. Try to include as many shapes as possible to provide interest e.g. sausage rolls, chicken twizzles, tuna baskets, mini-quiches, cream-cheese stars, stuffed cherry tomatoes, cheese and kiwi or cheese and grapes on sticks, cream horns, meringues, etc. Chefs often 'stack' food attractively on plates to add shape where there is none. Shaped plates can also add interest to plain food.

Presentation

One of the aims of a chef is to make food look (and taste) as appetising as possible. When thinking about presentation, you need to consider:

- consistency (how thin or how thick)
- texture (e.g. crunchy, soft, crisp)
- flavour (e.g. salty, sweet, sour, bitter, well-seasoned)
- seasoning (e.g. use of salt, pepper, herbs and spices)
- colour
- accompaniments (e.g. colourful vegetables and sauces)
- decoration (used on sweet dishes e.g. chocolate leaves, fresh fruit)
- garnish (used on savoury dishes e.g. parsley, tomatoes).

Do not over-season, over-decorate or over-fill dishes. The golden rule for all food presentation is keep it clean, neat, simple and colourful.

Garnishes should not be 'sprinkled' over dishes – the substance is difficult to remove if the customer does not like it.

Food that needs to be served hot should be hot (and not warm) and served on hot plates. Food that needs to be served cold should be served cold (but not frozen) and always on cold plates. Food probes can be used to check the temperature of food.

Savoury food is usually served in oval dishes or on oval plates with a dish paper (plain doiley) if needed. Sweet food is usually served in round dishes or on round plates with a sweet (pretty) doiley if needed.

ACTIVITY

You have trained as a chef and have set up your own contract catering business. You prepare and serve meals in clients' homes for special occasions. Choose one of the following assignments:

- Plan and if possible cook a lunch for a couple celebrating their first wedding anniversary.

- Design a menu for a Halloween party. Remember to think about foods in season.

- Working with a partner, plan a finger buffet for an 18th birthday party.

Halloween party
31st Oct
Start time 6.30
End time 10.00
Portland College

Planning a range of menus

What types of menu are available?

- Table d'hôte or set-price menu – a 'fixed' or set-price menu usually consists of two or three courses with a limited selection of dishes available at every course.
- À la carte menu – a menu where all the dishes are individually priced and cooked to order.
- Party or function menu – this type of menu can vary from drinks and canapés to a sit-down banquet for an event (e.g. wedding, anniversary, dinner dance, conference, meeting, corporate event). This type of menu usually has a fixed price and is often chosen beforehand (so that guests are not given a choice).
- Ethnic or speciality menu – this can be fixed price or à la carte. Speciality food of a particular country may be on offer (e.g. Chinese or Mexican) or the food itself could be specialised (e.g. fish, pasta, ice-cream, pancakes, pies, vegetarian.)
- Fast-food menu – this is similar in some ways to a speciality menu. It may have a theme like burgers, baked potatoes or fried chicken. All items are priced separately and 'finished' or cooked on demand.
- Rotating menu cycle – this is a 'fixed pattern' of menus that covers a 'fixed number' of days (called the menu cycle). The fixed number of days always includes a number of weeks plus 1 day (i.e. 8 days, 15 days, 22 days etc.). The addition of the extra day means that menu items are not repeated on the same day each week.

DESSERTS • HOT DRINKS

PLAIN CROISSANT	1.10	CAPPUCCINO	1.80
CHOC. CROISSANT	1.30	HOT CHOCOLATE	1.80
MUFFIN	1.30	CAFFE LATTE	1.80
DANISH	1.30	ESPRESSO	1.50
DOUGHNUT	1.30	COFFEE	1.30
CAKE SLICE	2.20	TEA	1.10
		EARL GREY TEA	1.30
WALKERS CRISPS	0.70	HERBAL TEA	1.30
JAM PORTION	0.25	FRESH MILK	0.90
BUTTER PORTION	0.20		

Other types of menu cater for people at work, patients in hospitals, school children and people who are travelling (e.g. on planes, trains, ferries, cruise ships)

> **ACTIVITY**
> Try to find examples of each type of menu. Local newspapers often have adverts for restaurants that offer table d'hôte, à la carte and party menus. Look out for take-away menus (e.g. Chinese, Indian or pizza). Find out if your local primary school offers a rotating menu.

Special dietary needs

Some people choose not to eat certain foods. There can be a variety of reasons for this:

- because of their ethical beliefs
- because of their religious beliefs
- for medical reasons
- they do not like the taste or texture of some foods.

Vegetarian diets

There are many reasons why people choose a vegetarian diet:

- They may have strong feelings about the way animals are kept and slaughtered.
- Land used to feed animals could feed many more if used for crops.
- Many cases of food poisoning are linked to meat.
- A vegetarian diet is considered to be healthier (lower in fat and cholesterol, higher in fibre) than one that relies on meat.

Many teenagers decide to become vegetarians.

There are three main categories of vegetarians:

1. Vegans do not eat the flesh of any animal (no meat, poultry or fish) and no eggs, milk, cheese, honey, etc.
2. Lacto-vegetarians do not eat the flesh of any animal (no meat, poultry or fish) but they do eat eggs, milk, cheese, honey etc.
3. Demi- or semi-vegetarians often choose to eat a mainly vegetarian diet because they don't eat red meat. They sometimes do eat white meat (poultry and fish) and eggs, milk, cheese, honey etc.

A vegetarian dish

Religious diets

Different religions have different dietary restrictions.
For example:

- Muslims do not eat pork (they believe the pig is an unclean animal). Meat has to be Halal (slaughtered in a special way according to their custom). They do not eat shellfish or drink alcohol.
- Hindus do not eat beef (they believe the cow is a sacred animal). Many are vegan, but some do eat lamb, poultry and/or fish.
- Some Sikhs eat all types of meat or fish. Others avoid meat and/or fish.
- Jews do not eat pork, bacon or ham, shellfish or eels. They do not eat meat or milk at the same time or cooked together (e.g. lasagne). They eat kosher meat (i.e. meat that has been prepared in accordance with Jewish dietary guidelines). Milk and milk products are usually eaten at breakfast only and avoided at other meals.
- Rastafarians do not eat processed foods (any food produced in a factory), pork or eels, or drink alcohol, tea or coffee.

Medical diets

There are many medical reasons why people cannot eat certain foods. They include diseases such as diabetes, allergies such as nut allergy and food intolerances such as gluten or lactose intolerance. With rising levels of people with obesity, high blood pressure and heart attacks, many people are advised to cut their fat, calorie, sugar and/or salt intake.

Some of these diets are outlined below:

- People with diabetes find it difficult to control their blood sugar levels, so need to eat starchy foods at regular intervals. They should avoid dishes that are high in sugar.
- People who are on a low-fat diet should avoid foods that are naturally high in fat e.g. cheese, bacon, butter, margarine, spreads and foods that are fried or roasted in fat.
- People who are on a low-salt diet should avoid most processed foods, smoked meats, cheese and Chinese foods containing monosodium glutamate.

Sugar-free chocolates for people with diabetes

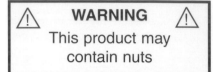

WARNING

This product may
contain nuts

- People who have a nut allergy must avoid nuts, blended cooking oils and margarines that contain nut oils. They must read food labels carefully – most state that foods 'may contain nuts' or have been 'prepared in an area that may contain nuts'.
- People who have lactose intolerance must avoid milk, cheese, butter, yogurt and processed foods that contain milk products. They must read food labels carefully.
- People who have a gluten intolerance (or coeliac disease) must avoid wheat, wholemeal, whole wheat and wheat meal flour, bran, pasta, noodles, semolina, bread, pastry, sauces thickened with flour, muesli, wheat, rye, barley and oat breakfast cereals, beer, and other malted drinks. However, they can eat rice, potatoes, corn and corn products. They must read food labels carefully.

Main courses

Steak and chips   £6.99
Prime Scottish steak and our famous chunky chips.
Cooked how you like it and served with your choice of pepper,
mushroom or blue cheese sauce.

Grilled salmon   £5.99
A fillet of wild salmon seasoned with cajun spices and grilled.
Served with new potatoes and seasonal vegetables.

V **Tomato and basil pasta**   £5.50
Fresh penne pasta in a rich tomato and basil sauce.
Served with garlic bread.

Chicken tikka masala   £5.99
A medium-hot curry made from an authentic recipe.
Served on basmati rice and accompanied with poppadoms
and mango chutney.

V **Spinach and goat's cheese bake**   £5.99
A burst of flavour from fresh spinach and goat's cheese,
wrapped in filo pastry and served with salad.

KEY WORDS:

Allergy: an adverse reaction by the body to certain substances (including foods).

Food intolerance: condition obliging someone to avoid a certain food because of the effect on their body.

Allgeric reaction: the way in which the body responds to some foods, for example: a rash, swelling and anaphylactic shock

ACTIVITY
How would you choose suitable dishes from this menu if you:

- are a vegetarian?
- suffer from diabetes?
- have a nut allergy?

Quality assurance and quality control are systems that are used within the hospitality and catering industry to ensure that customers have products and services that are of a consistent standard.

The best-known quality assurance systems are produced by the national tourist organisations for Britain (namely Visit Britain, Visit Wales and Visit Scotland) and the AA, where stars are awarded to establishments to show the quality of facilities and service they offer.

Restaurants are also involved in star ratings. Michelin stars are awarded every year to those providing an excellent standard of food and restaurants that are rated 'very good' or better feature *The Good Food Guide*.

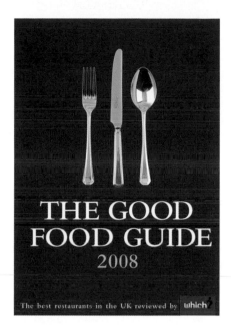

THE GOOD FOOD GUIDE 2008

The best restaurants in the UK reviewed by which

Croeso Cymru
Visit Wales

How do we judge quality?

The quality of a product or service can be difficult to define because it is determined (decided upon) by the customer's own perception (understanding or experience).

Products and services

When judging the quality of a product (such as a meal served in a restaurant), there are fewer variables to consider. Are the dishes beautifully cooked and presented, the correct consistency, well-seasoned? If the answer to all of these is 'yes', then the quality can be said to be good.

However, with a service (such as the serving of a meal in a restaurant), quality is more difficult to define. Research has found that customers judge the quality of service in many different ways. These are outlined below.

Reliability

Carrying out the service at the expected or appropriate time. This means that guests are not kept waiting. Hotel bills should be accurate so that guests do not have to question or challenge them. Accurate records are kept for any queries.

A beautifully presented tomato salad

Responding quickly to customers

Members of staff deal with customers willingly and promptly.

Competence

Members of staff have the skills and knowledge to carry out the service.

Accessibility

Members of staff are easily accessible. no matter what time of day or night it is. Staff are also approachable and friendly.

Courtesy

Members of staff are polite, considerate and friendly without being 'familiar'. Staff are also well-groomed and show respect to customers and their property.

Credibility

Members of staff are trustworthy and honest. Staff have the customers' well–being and enjoyment as their first concern.

Communication

Members of staff should be able to cater for different customers needs – this may involve addressing the customer's in their language, or simply by being clear and concise when dealing with problems and queries. Customers need to know that problems will be handled quickly and effectively.

Security

Customers need to be assured of their physical safety (to be free from danger or risk), to have financial security (e.g. their bank details secure) and confidentiality (other people should not have access to confidential information about them).

Meeting customer needs

Members of staff find out what the customer needs are, and meet or exceed these needs with good customer care. Staff should recognise 'regular' customers and make them feel welcome.

Other factors

Other factors that contribute to quality include the surroundings, the appearance of staff and the tools or equipment used to provide the service (this could be the plates used in a restaurant).

Quality will also be affected by other customers. If other customers are noisy or disorderly, it will affect people's enjoyment of a meal or their stay in a hotel.

Sometimes customers make up their minds about the quality of service they expect *before* they receive that service.

ACTIVITY

Imagine that you are going to McDonald's with a group of friends to buy a burger. What are you expecting of the service?

Imagine you are going to a wedding reception which is to be held in a four-star hotel. What are you expecting of the service?

Is it easy to imagine the different standards you would expect?

REMEMBER

Remember that service quality can be:
- Poor = does not meet expectations.
- Normal = as expected.
- Exceptional = exceeds expectations.

Accommodation ratings

The national tourism agency 'Visit Britain' is responsible for marketing Britain worldwide and for developing Britain's visitor economy. It has created new rating standards for accommodation. This includes hotels and guest accommodation, using stars to represent hotels and diamonds for guest accommodation, including guest houses, inns, farmhouses and bed-and-breakfast establishments. Self-catering accommodation and caravan parks are also represented by stars under the new system.

What to expect with each star rating

Five-star luxury hotels

These offer first-class services and accommodation with elegant and luxurious surroundings. The hotel restaurants often have famous chefs with a high standard of cuisine. Hotels are usually situated in desirable locations in major cities and resorts. Facilities include valet parking, concierge service, room service, well-equipped fitness centres and modern business centres.

Four-star deluxe hotels

These offer a comfort, class and quality that customers can rely on. The hotel will usually be situated in a prime location near to desirable shops and restaurants. Facilities may include valet parking, concierge service, room service, well equipped fitness centres and business centres.

Three-star mid-scale hotels

These are often situated near motorways, in city centres and suburbs. Rooms and reception areas are nicely furnished and offer a degree of comfort. Facilities may include swimming pools, fitness centres, room service and parking. There are restaurants within the hotels.

Two-star value hotels

These are often situated near office parks, airports, shopping and retail areas. Rooms are comfortably decorated but not elegant. Usually these hotels do not have restaurants or room service but offer free parking and sometimes a swimming pool. Transport may be available to nearby airports.

One-star economy hotels and motels

These are often situated near major motorways. They offer simple, basic accommodation. Facilities include free parking, cable TV and tea- and coffee-making in the rooms. Restaurants are often located nearby and room service is not available. Some economy hotels and motels have swimming pools

What to expect with each diamond rating

Five-diamond

These offer an excellent overall quality with plenty of space, high-quality furniture and excellent interior design. Breakfasts are fresh and often use seasonal, local ingredients when possible. There are excellent levels of customer care, anticipating customers' every need.

Four-diamond

These offer a very good overall level of quality, including comfortable bedrooms and a well maintained décor. Breakfasts offer a good choice of quality items, freshly cooked. There are very good levels of customer care, showing attention to customers' needs.

Three-diamond

These offer a good overall level of quality, including comfortable bedrooms and a well maintained, practical décor. Breakfasts offer a good choice of quality items, freshly cooked. There is a good level of comfort with good levels of customer care.

Two-diamond

These offer clean, comfortable accommodation with functional décor. Breakfasts may be continental or cooked. There is a sound level of quality and customer care in all areas.

A bedroom in a two-diamond hotel

One-diamond

These offer clean accommodation with an acceptable level of comfort and functional décor. Breakfasts may be continental or cooked. There is an acceptable level of quality and helpful service.

Self-catering

Properties have to provide the following before they can be considered for a star rating:

- a high standard of cleanliness throughout
- the prices and conditions of booking made clear
- local information provided so that customers make the most of their stay
- comfortable accommodation with a range of furniture to meet customer needs
- colour TV at no extra charge
- kitchen equipment to meet essential needs.

The more stars, the higher the overall quality. Once properties have met the minimum requirements, increased levels of quality then apply. Customers will find an acceptable level of quality at one-star, very good quality at three-star and exceptional quality at five-star.

Caravan parks

The star rating for caravan parks has been designed to reflect the quality and facilities that customers expect in caravan parks. A rating from one to five stars is awarded, based on cleanliness, environment and the quality of the facilities and service offered:

- one star - acceptable quality.
- two stars - good quality.
- three stars - very good quality.
- four stars - excellent quality.
- five stars - exceptional quality.

Accessibility

Not every customer has full mobility. VisitBritain's National Accessible Scheme places establishments in different categories of accessibility:

1. Accessible to someone who can climb a flight of stairs but would benefit from fixtures and fittings to aid balance.
2. Accessible to someone with restricted walking ability who is able to walk up a maximum of three steps.
3. Accessible to someone who depends on a wheelchair but transfers to and from the wheelchair unaided.
4. Accessible to someone who depends on a wheelchair and needs assistance.
5. Exceptional access for independent wheelchair users.
6. Exceptional access for independent wheelchair users and those who need assistance.

Establishments that have been rated will display National Accessible Scheme symbols.

DESIGN AND LAYOUT OF WORK ENVIRONMENTS

Modern trends in planning and design mean that many restaurants have their kitchen areas in view. In the same way, modern hotels have the different areas of the hotel close together, so that they are easily accessible for customers and staff, and also save money and fuel.

The different areas

The entrance

A guest's experience of staying in a hotel starts at the entrance. The grounds and entrance provide important clues as to the type of hotel it is, so these need to reflect the style of the interior.

> **ACTIVITY**
>
> Look at the entrances to these hotels – do they all look like hotels?
>
> Explain why they do, or do not.
>
> What would your expectations of each hotel be?
>
> Clues: Hotels may be budget, luxurious, traditional, and either commercial (i.e. for the business traveller) or for leisure.

Reception areas

The reception area of a hotel is often said to be the 'nerve centre' of the hotel. It is the first contact point with the customer and often the last. The saying 'you only have one chance to make a first impression' is especially true of the reception area and staff. The reception desk needs to be seen clearly from the entrance. To improve security, the desk should be positioned so that staff can keep an eye on the whole area.

Factors that influence reception design include:

- the size of the hotel
- the number of staff

- the need for security
- the décor /image required e.g. hotel groups often have recognisable features which are the same in every hotel
- the space available – customers often wait in reception areas for friends to arrive, taxis to collect them etc.
- the need for a large enough reception area to deal with the volume of customers that book in at any one time
- access for computer terminal points
- the need to be warm and welcoming
- the level of comfort needed – the higher the star rating the higher the level of comfort provided
- the type of customer who uses the hotel
- well-signed access to bedrooms, the restaurant and other areas of the hotel.

Accommodation areas

Bedrooms in hotels may vary in style, but generally they are very similar. Guests require a bed, somewhere to hang or store their clothes, a bedside cabinet and some form of luggage storage. If bedrooms have en-suite bathrooms, these should contain a toilet, a hand basin, a shower and/or bath.

Designs of bedrooms can vary from fun to vivid, colourful to brash and unique to quaint. Some rural (country) hotels like to create the atmosphere of a luxury country house to attract foreign visitors. Some city centre hotels ensure guests have all the facilities they need to carry on their business from their hotel room.

Factors that influence the design of accommodation areas include:

- the type of hotel (budget, luxurious, traditional, commercial (for the business guest) a leisure centre, etc.)
- corporate identity – an identical design may be used by every hotel in a particular chain
- the level of comfort needed
- the level of facilities and services needed.

Restaurant areas

Hotel guests do not always want a large meal in a formal restaurant. Larger hotels may have several restaurants that vary in level of formality and the type and price of menu offered. Some hotels have bars serving coffee and light snacks. These offer a good alternative to full meals and can also be used to attract non-residents to the hotel.

The interior design of a restaurant (i.e. the colours and finishes, the furnishings, the lighting and layout) all work together to create a particular atmosphere. Guests often like to eat in interesting and different surroundings. Large hotels often give their restaurants a distinctive flavour or theme. The more unusual a restaurant is, the more likely guests are to tell their friends about it.

Factors that influence the design of the restaurant/eating areas include:

- the sort of menu that is on offer
- the sort of service that is needed – self service or waited service
- how the food and drink is displayed or served
- the facilities (food display counter, bar area, etc.) that will be needed
- how many staff will be needed.

Breakfast in a hotel restaurant

Kitchen areas

Before a kitchen is planned, several factors need to be considered, including the type of customer, the menu and style of food service. Kitchens should be designed so that they are easy to manage in terms of efficiency and hygiene. It is a good idea to have a flow of work through the kitchen, from delivery – storage – prep – cooking – chilling – hot-holding – serving – washing up – refuse disposal.

Factors that influence kitchen design include:

- the amount of money available to spend
- whether the kitchen is 'new-build' or a refit
- the space available
- the size of the food service area and number of covers needed
- the style of food service (e.g. a carvery service has different needs to fast-food service)
- the proximity (nearness) of the food service area
- services available – gas, electricity and water
- staff skills

- the menu to be offered – using pre-prepared meals or a lot of convenience foods will require fewer staff and less equipment
- the equipment available
- where equipment is situated (large items of equipment already 'in situ' may be impossible to move)
- storage areas
- legislation – kitchens must conform to Food Hygiene Regulations, the Food Safety Act etc.

Multi-usage requirements

Some establishments, such as hospitals and factories, have peak times when the whole of the kitchen area needs to be used. They also have quiet times when only a small number of people require food and drink. Modern kitchens are planned to be more adaptable, so that whole sections can be closed down when not in use. This means that unused sections do not need heating or lighting. Multi-use kitchens therefore save money and are kinder to the environment.

Looking after the environment is really important to help prevent global warming. The hospitality and catering industry has a part to play in this, by reducing the amount of waste it produces and by recycling as much as possible.

In hospitality and catering, there are three 'Rs' that relate to looking after the environment. These are:

- reduce
- reuse
- recycle.

What the industry can do

How can hotels reduce the amount of waste within the kitchens?

- Using products with less packaging.
- Sending waste food to local farmers, for animal feed.
- Buying foods in bulk.
- Recycling glass, tins, cardboard and paper.

Restaurants can reduce waste at breakfast time (and save money) by:

- running a buffet-style breakfast (that way, people will only take what they like and fewer members of staff will be needed)
- putting condiments such as jam in dishes, rather than providing individual ones (which cost more and produce more waste).

Hotels can reduce waste and save money when providing toiletries in the guest rooms by:

- providing large bottles of shampoo and shower gel that are fixed to the wall and can be re-filled.
- providing a smaller range of toiletries in every room.

Hotels and guest houses can also reduce waste and save money by:

- asking guests to use the towels more than once. Many use signs saying 'If you want a clean towel please put the dirty one in the bath and we will replace it.' By

reusing the towels, guests help to cut down on the use of water and electricity.
- providing showers rather baths, which reduces the amount of water used.

There are now a range of things some hotels no longer provide for guests. These include: shoe-cleaning kits, sewing kits, shower caps, individual soaps, laundry service.

Packaging

We use packaging for food to:

- protect the contents
- hold the contents
- keep it fresh
- reduce waste
- make food easier to handle, transport and serve
- improve hygiene
- make the contents look more attractive
- give information on the contents, storage and use.

> **KEY WORDS:**
>
> The hospitality and catering industry can play a big part in helping the environment by following three 'Rs':
> Reduce, Reuse AND Recycle.

Types of packaging

Packaging	Advantages	Disadvantages
Paper and card	Easily printed. Can be recycled. Strong when dry. Lightweight.	Crushes easily. Weak when wet. Recycled paper and card cannot be used for food.
Glass	Easily printed. Strong. Reusable. Recyclable. Can carry liquids.	Brittle. Easily broken.
Metal	Recyclable. Easily printed. Strong. Rigid.	Must be coated inside or reacts with food. Cannot microwave. Uses valuable energy to extract from ground.
Plastic and polystyrene	Strong. Flexible. Easily printed. Does not react with food.	Causes litter problem. Limited resource. Not easily recycled.

Take-away food establishments in particular use a lot of packaging. For example, pizzas are sold in corrugated card boxes, sandwiches are often sold in clear plastic boxes, many Indian and Chinese foods are sold in plastic containers or foil containers with card lids and burgers are sold in polystyrene cartons.

Food manufacturers are trying to reduce the amount of packaging used for food products. Customers are encouraged to reuse and recycle food packaging whenever possible.

ACTIVITY

In the picture below, a bin has been knocked over and everything has spilled out. Look carefully at the picture and see how many items you can identify that could be recycled or re-used. Then describe how they can be recycled or re-used. (For example, grass cuttings can be put on the compost and used as fertilizer for the gardens once they have rotted.)

Reduce

Recycle   Reuse

The hospitality and catering industry can do their part in helping to reduce waste produced by themselves and their customers. By putting signs around the establishment encouraging customers to help reduce waste they will in turn gain a good reputation, as they are trying to help the environment.

REMEMBER

Remember the three Rs: reduce, re-use, recycle.

Food Safety Act (1990)

The Food Safety Act covers food safety from raw ingredients through to finished products. The law concentrates on making sure food is safe to eat and is of the quality and composition that customers expect. The Act gives Environmental Health officers the power to:

- enter any food premises at any time
- inspect food
- take samples of food away for analysis
- take any food they judge to be unfit
- ask a Justice of the Peace (JP) to condemn food which is unsafe
- give 'improvement notices' to food businesses
- close premises down.

The Food Safety Act links closely with Hazard Analysis Critical Control Points (HACCP) and Food Hygiene Regulations. The Act emphasises the need for a high level of personal hygiene amongst staff, good hygiene habits of staff, avoiding cross contamination, safe storage of food, good cleaning schedules and strict temperature controls. Under the Act food handlers and manufacturers may be prosecuted if their food is found to be unsafe to eat.

HACCP

HACCP stands for (Hazard Analysis Critical Control Points). It is now a legal requirement for all food businesses to carry out some form of hazard analysis to identify the most critical (dangerous in terms of bacteria) areas of their business and to make sure they are under control.

Hazards

A hazard is something that has the potential to cause harm. In the food industry, hazards include those shown in the table overleaf.

Type of hazard	Example
Biological	Salmonella in chicken
Chemical	Contamination from cleaning materials e.g. bleach
Physical	Damaged packaging, glass found in food

Physical and chemical damage can often be seen. Food contaminated with bacteria however can look, smell and taste perfectly normal.

Critical control points

There are areas in the food business where control is *essential* to reduce the risk of food poisoning. If a caterer 'gets it wrong' they could be breaking the law, so it is important to ensure every step from the purchasing of food through its preparation and serving is controlled.

Food Safety (General Food Hygiene) Regulations (1995)

These regulations cover three main areas.

- food premises
- personal hygiene of staff
- hygienic practices.

ACTIVITY
Choose a food (e.g. frozen chicken breasts). Fill in the chart below, stating what the hazards/ dangers might be at every stage and stating what action you would take to ensure your customers do not suffer from salmonella food poisoning.

HACCP CHART		
Food	**Hazard**	**Action**
Buying		
Delivery		
Storage		
Preparation		
Cooking		
Cooling		

Food Labelling Regulations (2006)

By law, the following information should be on a label:

- 'use by' or 'best before' date
- list of ingredients in weight order, with the heaviest first
- name of manufacturer
- address of manufacturer
- name of the food and a brief description of the food (if it is not obvious)
- weight (the 'e' symbol shows average weight of similar packets) barcode – shows where and when manufactured and price
- special claims about the food (suitable for vegetarians, low in fat)
- method of storage, making, cooking.

Food manufacturers often include nutritional information, but report on fat, carbohydrate (starch with sugars), fibre and total kcal (energy value) only. Often vitamins and minerals are not included. There is continuing debate about the best way of giving nutritional information on food.

RIDDOR (1995)

RIDDOR stands for Reporting of Injuries, Diseases and Dangerous Occurences Regulations. Reporting accidents and ill-health at work is a legal requirement. All employers have a duty under the regulations to report incidents at work.

What needs to be reported?

Al of the following should be reported:

- deaths
- major injuries
- accidents resulting in over a three-day injury
- diseases – these include skin diseases such as dermatitis, which could be caused by cleaning chemicals; asthma, which could be aggravated by working in a dusty environment; and infections such as tetanus, Legionnaires' disease and tuberculosis (TB)
- dangerous occurrences (happenings)
- gas incidents.

Who is the report made to?

All accidents, diseases and dangerous occurrences may be reported to the Incident Contact Centre, which was established in April 2001 as the main contact centre for all incidents in the UK. The incident centre is located in Caerphilly, South Wales.

If the business is one of the following, details of the incident will be given to the Environmental Health Department of the Local Authority.

- hotel and catering
- sports or leisure
- mobile vending
- residential accommodation
- pre-school child care
- office based
- warehousing
- place of worship.

What records need to be kept?

The following records should be kept:

- the date, time and place of event
- the personal details of those involved
- a brief description of the nature of the event or disease
- the date and method of reporting the injury, disease or dangerous occurrence.

COSHH (2002)

COSHH stands for Control of Substances Hazardous to Health. There are many substances, particularly those used during cleaning, that could damage health. These substances are recognised and labelled as:

- very toxic (poisonous)
- toxic harmful
- irritant
- corrosive.

What effects can hazardous substances have?

Incorrect use of hazardous substances can cause:

- skin irritation or dermatitis as a result of contact with the skin
- asthma as a result of developing an allergy to substances used at work
- losing consciousness as a result of being overcome by toxic (poisonous) fumes
- cancer – which may appear a long time after a person has been exposed to the chemical that caused it
- infection from bacteria and other micro-organisms.

To comply (meet with) COSHH, employers need to follow the eight steps in the table below.

Step 1	Assess the risks	Assess the risks to health from the hazardous substances used in the workplace.
Step 2	Decide what precautions are needed	Do not carry out work which could endanger employees without first considering the risks.
Step 3	Prevent or control exposure	Where preventing (stopping) exposure to hazardous substances is not possible, the exposure must be controlled.
Step 4	Control measures are used and maintained	All control measures are used and maintained properly. Safety procedures are followed.
Step 5	Monitor the exposure	Keep records of all exposure to hazardous substances.
Step 6	Carry out regular health checks	Carry out regular health checks on employees especially when COSHH sets specific requirements.
Step 7	Have plans and procedures to deal with accidents, incidents and emergencies	Prepare plans and procedures to deal with accidents, incidents and emergencies where necessary.
Step 8	Ensure employees are properly informed, trained and supervised	All employers should provide suitable and sufficient information, instruction and training.

Other legislation

Licensing laws

Premises that want to sell alcohol need to obtain a Justices License. There are several types of license:

- restaurant license – this is given to restaurants who want to sell alcohol before, during and after food service.
- residential license – this is given to premises that provide board and lodging e.g. guest houses, hotels and inns.
- combined license – this combines Restaurant and Residential licenses. It is given to businesses that offer board and lodging but also have separate function rooms (e.g. conference facilities, large reception rooms for weddings etc.).
- off-license – this is a license that allows alcohol to be sold for consumption 'off' or 'away from' the premises.
- occasional licenses – these are granted on an irregular basis to allow large functions to sell alcohol e.g. for dances, wedding receptions held in village halls etc.

Fair trading, trades description and trading standards

The 'Trades Description Act' makes it a criminal offence to 'falsely describe' goods or services. Care must be taken when:

- wording the menu (e.g. frozen foods cannot be called fresh)
- describing menu items to customers
- letting customers know about extra costs e.g. service charges
- describing service conditions.

Health and Safety at Work Act (1974)

This covers all aspects of health and safety at work. All employers must provide safe working areas. All employees must take care of their own health and safety and not endanger others.

Examples of questions and answers

This section gives some examples of the kinds of questions you will have to answer in your written exam. It is always a good idea to try several past questions so that you can see how the questions are set out and what kind of responses you are expected to give. By doing this you increase your chances of getting a good mark.

This section in two parts:

- Part 1 gives two long questions, each with a candidate's example answers. Mark schemes are provided at the end of each question.
- Part 2 gives a set of shorter example questions, with the number of marks available shown in brackets after each one. A detailed mark scheme for the questions is given at the end of the section.

Mark schemes

The mark schemes show what the examiner will expect you to say in your answers. They are broken down into sections, and show how many marks are possible for a list, a simple answer and a detailed, clear answer.

Part 1

The answers to Questions 1 and 2 (below) did not gain full marks. However, they are classed as good responses.

> **ACTIVITY**
>
> Have a look at Questions 1 and 2 and the answers that the candidate gave.
>
> Can you think of anything that is missing? How would you have answered the question?
>
> Read through the relevant sections of the book to help you. Have a go *before* you look at the mark scheme.

> **REMEMBER** ✔
>
> Remember that the questions that come later in the exam paper require long and detailed answers, not just a list. It is a good idea to highlight key words in longer questions to help you to focus when you are writing your answer.

ACTIVITY

Try to work out how many marks you think the candidate would get for each part of their answer, and give your reasons why.

Question 1

Elen and Troy are opening a new restaurant in a large city. They want to target the young professionals who work in the city, as well as the visiting tourists. They plan to serve food from 11 a.m. until 9 p.m.

They want a modern restaurant with a semi open-plan kitchen, which will be visible to the customers. Customers will be able to see their dishes being freshly and quickly prepared.

a) Discuss the main points to consider when planning the choice of foods for the menu. (6)

CANDIDATE'S ANSWER

When Elen and Troy open their new restaurant their menu needs to be carefully planned to ensure that they reach the needs of their target customers 'young professionals who work in the city'. The design and layout of the menu needs to be accurate to appeal to these customers. The choice of dishes served needs to vary from meat to vegetarians. Meals such as 'burger and chips' could be sold, but altered to ensure that they are healthy. The restaurant should supply both à la carte and table d'hôte menus as younger customers may prefer a set price menu which is easy and affordable. Lunchtime meals such as toasted panini served with chips, or scampi and chips would be an easy but effective dish to sell. Dietary needs need to be taken into consideration, so customers who suffer from a nut allergy or wheat allergy need to be taken into consideration. Also people of different ethnic minorities such as Asian or Chinese need a choice of meal to choose from, so noodles or chicken tikka masala could be dishes to take into consideration.

b) Assess the importance of a well-planned kitchen. (10)

CANDIDATE'S ANSWER

It is important that the layout of the kitchen is well planned for a number of different reasons. If Elen and Troy want a semi-open kitchen in which their customers can see their dishes being cooked and prepared, they need to make sure that there is good organisation and that the appliances are kept clean at all times and are easy to access. Appliances need to be accurately laid out, for example the washing up area would not be good planned near where food is being prepared as this would give the wrong impression to the customer as it would look like poor health and hygiene. Although the kitchen needs to be equipped with most large industrial size appliances, they need to be kept to a minimum to ensure that the kitchen looks presentable and clutter free. The kitchen needs to be accessible to members of staff, so doorways and fire exits must be kept clear. Delivery points need to always be taken into consideration when planning the kitchen. Elen and Troy want their customers to see their food being cooked so an industrial hob needs to be fitted accurately not too close to the customers as it would be a health risk. The right safety equipment needs to be fitted into the kitchen, e.g. fire extinguishers and fire blankets so it meets the expectations of the EHO officer.

c) Elen and Troy need staff to work in both the food preparation and service area of the restaurant. Discuss the qualities and skills staff will need to be employed in this type of open-plan restaurant.

CANDIDATE'S ANSWER

If Elen and Troy want their staff to work in both food preparation and service their employees will need to be equipped with a number of different skills, the first one being good communication and social skills. They will need to be able to take directions from fellow chefs within the kitchen, but also be able to approach and communicate with their customers in the restaurant. The second skill which will be required is good knowledge of health and hygiene because if they are walking to and from the kitchen they could pick up and spread a large amount of bacteria. Things such as hair tied back and regular washing of hands must be kept to strictly to ensure that there is no contamination of food. Employees must also be conscious of their surroundings as most of the time they will probably be in a rush to meet the customers' needs, so they need to be aware of wet floors etc and get them labelled. Employees need to have skills in all areas of the restaurant and need to know how to operate all the technology and appliances such as the till or electric hobs. They need a good sense of time keeping and need to know when each dish is ready to be served as customers can see and will be waiting for their meal to be cooked. If an employee knows that there is an expected delivery they need to ensure that this is collected and stored in a fast manner so it does not disturb people's meals. Members of staff need to be able to work a kitchen and service rota so there is no confusion about where they are working on that day. They also need to be aware of the Health and Safety at Work Act and that the policy is up to date. Members of staff need to be calm under pressure as a restaurant in a city will get very busy.

Mark scheme for Question 1

a) Answer could include:

- Nutritionally balanced diet.
- Variety of colour, flavour and texture.
- Foods in season.
- Time of year.
- Skills of chef.
- Type of outlet.
- Cost.
- Suitability and appeal to client.
- Time available.
- Latest food trends.

Award 5–6 marks for an answer that recalls detailed knowledge and demonstrates a comprehensive and detailed understanding of menu planning. The answer will include a wide range of points with evidence of detailed discussion. The response is well structured and clearly expressed with few errors.

Award 3–4 marks for an answer that recalls knowledge and demonstrates understanding of menu planning. The answer will include a range of points with evidence of discussion. Expression is adequate to convey meaning but some errors may be apparent.

Award 1–2 marks for an answer that recalls some knowledge and demonstrates a basic knowledge of menu planning. The answer may be a simple list or restricted number of suggestions. Communication will tend to be impeded by poor expression.

b) Answer could include:

- Layout.
- Lighting.
- Materials used.
- Size and extent of the menu it serves.
- Services – gas, electricity, water.
- Amount of capital.
- Types of equipment available.
- Amount of time to be spent using the kitchen.
- The golden triangle: fridge, cooker, sink.
- Separate areas for preparation.
- Hygiene and Food Safety Acts.
- Hand-washing facilities.

Award 7–10 marks for an answer that recalls detailed knowledge and demonstrates a comprehensive and detailed understanding of kitchen planning. The answer will include a wide range of points with evidence of detailed discussion. The response is well structured and clearly expressed with few errors.

Award 4–6 marks for an answer that recalls knowledge and demonstrates understanding of kitchen planning. The answer will include a range of points with evidence of discussion. Expression is adequate to convey meaning but some errors may be apparent.

Award 1–3 marks for an answer that recalls some knowledge and demonstrates a basic knowledge of kitchen planning. The answer may be a simple list or restricted number of suggestions. Communication will tend to be impeded by poor expression.

c) Answer could include:

- Good customer skills.
- Team member.
- Excellent communication skills.
- Qualifications in Hospitality and Catering.
- Clean.
- Smart appearance.
- Friendly.
- Knowledge and Certificate in Hygiene.
- Knowledge of special diets.

Award 7–10 marks for an answer that recalls detailed knowledge and demonstrates a comprehensive and detailed understanding of qualities and skills required. The answer will include a wide range of points with evidence of detailed discussion. The response is well structured and clearly expressed with few errors.

Award 4–6 marks for an answer that recalls knowledge and demonstrates understanding of qualities and skills required. The answer will include a range of points with evidence of discussion. Expression is adequate to convey meaning but some errors may be apparent.

Award 1–3 marks for an answer that recalls some knowledge and demonstrates a basic knowledge of qualities and skills required. The answer may be a simple list or restricted number of suggestions. Communication will tend to be impeded by poor expression.

Question 2:

Following recent government guidelines, fast food outlets are offering a more varied choice on their menus.

a) State three reasons why we should have a healthy diet.

(3)

> **CANDIDATE'S ANSWER**
>
> i) Reduce the risk of obesity in children and young people.
> ii) Keep the body functioning properly e.g. keeping eyes strong.
> iii) Lower the risk of heart diseases as we get older.

b) Explain how fast food outlets can make their food interesting and healthy to attract more customers. (6)

> **CANDIDATE'S ANSWER**
>
> Healthy food means having a balance of protein, fat and carbohydrates. Fast food outlets can provide this but they need to advertise well to sell. For younger children they can create a cartoon animal to set an example by eating the healthy foods. If children see bright colourful characters eating foods they will want to follow. Often famous people are used to attract teenagers and adults. The food can be made more interesting by adding new flavours and dressings. More colour and variety in foods. For example rather than beef burgers make minted lamb burgers or pork and apple burgers. Offer a range of dressings or sauces, salads and cheeses. Also they must create a more vegetarian friendly menu using meat alternatives, beans, peas and lentils to attract more vegetarian customers. They then have to advertise well to inform people of the new menu available.

c) Suggest ways in which a burger bar could offer alternatives for vegetarians that are both healthy and tasty. (6)

> **CANDIDATE'S ANSWER**
>
> A burger bar can adapt the products it sells to suit vegetarian needs easily. They can provide 'veggie' burgers as many already do but they can also introduce meat alternatives such as tofu, soya and quorn. These are all suitable alternatives for vegetarians. Also they could offer lentils, peas and beans in soups or stews. The burger vans also need to consider vegans who do not eat any dairy products either. This means they cannot offer cheese or milk in two or more products to make them suitable for vegans. As vegetarians do not eat meat it is important they

get protein and other essential food groups from the foods they eat. This is why lentils and beans are good. They are high in protein and provide a great source for an alternative menu. If the burger bar wanted to expand more they could offer salads and seafood options.

Mark scheme for Question 2

a) Any three of the following:

- prevent heart disease
- prevent obesity
- reduces high levels of cholesterol
- minimise risk of high blood pressure
- prevent tooth decay
- live longer, more active lifestyle

1 mark for each correct answer.

b) Methods of cooking, grilling instead of frying:

- offer low fat alternatives
- use less processed food
- offer healthy drinks, yoghurt or milk based, flavoured water
- offer interesting salads and vegetable dishes
- wraps instead of burgers
- sweeteners instead of sugar
- healthy choices for kids e.g. vegetable sticks and fruit
- add herbs and spices instead of salt
- promotional offers on new products such as wraps
- low-fat dressings on salads.

Award 1–2 marks for an answer that recalls some knowledge and demonstrates a basic knowledge of how to make foods healthier. The answer may be a simple list or restricted number of suggestions. Communication will tend to be impeded by poor expression.

Award 3–4 marks for an answer that recalls knowledge and demonstrates understanding of how to make foods healthier. The answer will include a range of points with evidence of discussion. Expression is adequate to convey meaning but some errors may be apparent.

Award 5–6 marks for an answer that recalls detailed knowledge and demonstrates a comprehensive and detailed understanding of how to make foods healthier. The answer will include a wide range of points with evidence of detailed discussion. The response is well structured and clearly expressed with few errors.

c) Use of quorn, tofu, veggie burgers, wraps. Added flavour with spices and herbs or by adding a sauce to the product.

Award 1–2 marks for an answer that recalls some knowledge and demonstrates a basic knowledge of how to make vegetarian alternatives. The answer may be a simple list or restricted number of suggestions. Communication will tend to be impeded by poor expression.

Award 3–4 marks for an answer that recalls knowledge and demonstrates understanding of how to make vegetarian alternatives. The answer will include a range of points with evidence of discussion. Expression is adequate to convey meaning but some errors may be apparent.

Award 5–6 marks for an answer that recalls detailed knowledge and demonstrates a comprehensive and detailed understanding of how to make vegetarian alternatives The answer will include a wide range of points with evidence of detailed discussion. The response is well structured and clearly expressed with few errors.

Part 2

Try to answer the following questions. The amount of marks for each question is given in brackets. Have a go before you look at the mark scheme. When you have completed the answer, check the mark scheme to see what you may have missed and how the marks are given.

1. You are working for a firm of Contract Caterers who have been asked to prepare and serve a meal for an engagement party.
   a) What do you understand by the term contract caterers? (2)
   b) Hazard Analysis and Critical Control Points are important when preparing and serving food for the occasion.
   Identify and explain **four** safety checks that are critical to the safe preparation and serving of food. (4)

2. A catering firm is planning to offer a party service for children.
   a) Plan a suitable menu including **two** savoury dishes, **one** sweet dish and a drink. (4)
   b) Discuss points the catering firm must consider when planning a suitable party menu. (6)
   c) Describe how the caterer could make the table and room look attractive for the party. (3)

3. a) Describe the qualities and or skills needed by a head chef in a large restaurant. (4)
   b) Discuss the role the restaurant manager has in the running of the hotel restaurant. (4)

4. Record keeping is important and helps to ensure the smooth running of the hotel industry.
   a) Explain why the following types of record keeping are used in the reception area of a hotel. (5)
      i) Room Lists
      ii) Booking forms
      iii) Customer Telephone bills
      iv) Customer Survey
      v) Restaurant Orders
   b) Explain why stock control records are used in the kitchen. (3)

5) Jacky and Nicky have recently taken over a busy country pub specializing in evening meals and Sunday lunches. They intend to refurbish the kitchen area as it is badly planned making it unhygienic and difficult to work in.
   a) Discuss the factors which influence the planning and design of the new kitchen area. (4)
   b) Before the kitchen can be used the local EHO will make a visit. Explain the role of the EHO within the kitchen area. (4)
   c) What advice could the EHO give Jacky and Nicky on the training of staff for their new kitchen? (2)

Mark scheme for Part 2

1. a) Award **1** mark for simple list or single comment that reflects some knowledge of the role of contract caterer.

   Award **2** marks for answer which lists one or more of the above or is descriptive in content.

   The role of contract caterer could include the following points:

- Has overall responsibility for organisation of event working to information given by the customer.
- Complete all administration for food for the event including ordering food, arranging the chef to cook the meal beforehand.
- Arranging the wait staff to serve the food on the day, these could be agency staff so the contract caterer would have to liaise with the agency.
- Organise along with the customer where the event will be held, liaise with the manager at the venue.
- Organise table layouts for service.
- Set the standards for service.
- Co-operate with chef in menu planning.
- Liaise with the customer throughout the planning of the event and ensure that the customers wishes are met fully.
- Hold meeting before service to ensure smooth running of meal and solve any problems that may occur.

b) **1 mark** for four points with no detail for reasons or if they only refer to one safety check e.g. personal hygiene or risk assessment.

2–3 marks for list that shows some knowledge and understanding of HACCP and how to prevent with little description.

4 marks. For a well written answer that reflects the knowledge and understanding of HACCP with detailed description of all relevant areas with clear explanation. For full marks they should correctly identify temperature zones.

Answer could include:

- Checks on purchase of goods, dates and quality- to ensure food is safe to eat.
- Safe storage of food before, during and after preparation with temperature of fridges etc.
- Use of different chopping boards, knives etc – colours as examples could be given, therefore avoiding cross contamination.
- Cooling of prepared foods, rapidly to 1–4°C – to prevent bacterial growth.
- Use of blast chillers to cool food rapidly – to prevent bacterial growth.

- Checking temperature of fridges/freezers.
- Checking core temperature of cooked meats 72°C – to ensure they are working correctly.
- Personal hygiene (only allow one e.g. hands washed, whites worn).
- Safe reheating of foods to core temperature of 72°C – use of temperature probe.
- Minimal time in danger zone. Food served quickly. 37 – 63°C.

2. a) Allow **1** mark for **each** suitable item.

Savoury – named sandwiches, dips, pizzas, pastry dish, fast food option. (Must include a protein food), pasta option, jacket potato option, sausages, curry and rice.

Sweet – mousse, fruit jelly, fresh fruit salad, trifle, biscuits, gateau, ice cream, named cakes, jam tarts.

Drink – smoothies, milkshakes, fruit juices, fizzy drinks, **no** alcohol.

b) Possible points discussed.

Point	Discussion
Food costs	Bulk buying will help reduce production cost.
Where food is to be served	Location of venue, facilities for storing dishes at correct temperature.
How the food is to be served	Buffet, plate service, wait service, seating arrangements, portion size.
Age of the children	Menu must be appropriate to the age group. Likes and dislikes.
Kitchen facilities	It is possible to assemble some dishes on site. Number of fridges, is there a freezer? Oven for hot food.
Operating costs	Must include labour costs, wear and tear of equipment, fuel, travelling, number to cater for.
Season	Hot or cold food. Using food in season helps reduce food costs.
Contrast in flavour, texture and appearance.	A variety will provide a more balanced meal and make food more interesting and appetising. Nutritional balance
Special diet	Vegetarian/allergy/cultural needs

Allow **1–2 marks** for basic principles discussed. Possible reference made to only 1 or 2 of the above points, bullet points only. Answer may resemble a list with no discussion.

Allow **3–4 marks** for answers where candidates will have discussed any of the above points. Some understanding of menu planning evident.

Allow **5–6 marks** for a very good answer. Candidates will have discussed most of the above points. Showing a good understanding of menu planning.

c) Allow up to 3 marks for any suitable suggestions on how to make table/room attractive.

Answers could include:
- Seating arrangements/ place names. Size of chairs/tables.
- Toys/games/activities.
- Balloons/banners/hats/poppers/posters.
- Lighting i.e. Halloween.
- Themes e.g. Thomas the Tank Engine.
- Paper table cloths- colourful cups, plates (plastic/paper).
- Party bags.
- Music.
- Birthday cards/presents displayed.
- Decorations must be specific.

3. a) Answers should include:

- The chef should have the relevant qualifications – City and Guilds, BTec, in-house or any professional training as it identifies the knowledge of the chef.
- Should have knowledge of a range or recipes developed from experience.
- Should be able to work well under pressure.
- Should have a good palate to know what foods go well together.
- Be able to produce meals with limited ingredients in case food orders do not arrive.
- Should have knowledge of stock control as they are responsible for the budget and costing and are responsible to the manager to make a profit.
- Should have knowledge and qualifications in food safety and hygiene.

- Should be a team leader, have clear leadership skills, have good communication skills and relate well to others as they are responsible for the staff.

Award 1–2 marks for an answer that reflects some knowledge and a basic understanding of the qualities of a good head chef. The answer may just resemble a list. 1 mark only for repetition or limited answer.

Award 3–4 marks for a well written answer that reflects knowledge and understanding of the qualities and skills required to be a good head chef. Reasons should be given.

b) Answer could include the following.:

- Has overall responsibility for the organisation of the restaurant and solves any problems which may arise.
- Sets the standards for service within the restaurant.
- Complete all administration for food and beverage service areas.
- Organises banquets and functions.
- Organises table layouts for service.
- Solves any problems with staff rotas, holidays etc.
- Organises training for staff.
- Completes duty rotas and holiday lists.
- Holds meetings to ensure the smooth running of areas and service.
- Co-operates with the chef when planning menus.
- Updates wine lists.
- Liaises with wine waiters.
- Liaise with staff and informs them when foods are running low or no longer available.
- Liaise with reception/ booking desk to ensure restaurant is not overbooked for service.
- Takes bookings for meals.

Award 1–2 marks for an answer that recalls some knowledge and demonstrates a basic knowledge of the role of restaurant manager. The answer may be a simple list or restricted number of suggestions. Communication will tend to be impeded by poor expression.

Award 3–4 marks for an answer that recalls knowledge and demonstrates understanding of the role of restaurant manager. The answer may relate to a limited number of points with evidence of discussion. Expression is adequate to convey meaning but some errors may be apparent. They may discuss one area in detail and only list other areas

Award 5–6 marks for an answer that recalls detailed knowledge and demonstrates a comprehensive and detailed understanding of the role of restaurant manager. The answer will include a wide range of points with evidence of detailed discussion. The response is well structured and clearly expressed with few errors.

Do not credit answers where discussion relates to hotel manager or chef.

4. 1 mark for each detailed correct answer.

i) This enables the receptionist to pass the information on to the housekeeper and she can then check the rooms are ready for use. The housekeeper will also know which rooms are becoming vacant and need cleaning each day. It also enables the receptionist to allocate any rooms available to customers.

ii) The receptionist will know what rooms and function rooms are available for hire and when. They will have this information to hand when dealing with enquiries on the phone. This helps with the smooth running of the hotel.

iii) This allows the customer's bills to be made up ready for when they check out. Itemised bills ensure the customer knows what they are being charged for and when calls were made.

iv) A customer survey helps the Hotel/Restaurant to make sure they do the best they can. Customer feedback is a good way of finding out what the customer wants and how service can be improved. Any problems that may have occurred will be highlighted by the customer.

v) This enables the receptionist to work out the customer's bill, by telling them what food the customer has eaten and how much it costs. It also enables the restaurant manger to check the correct foods have been served. This can be cross referenced with the kitchen copy to check on meals served and stock held.

b) Stock Control records are used in the kitchen so that the chefs can see at a glance what stock needs to be ordered to produce the meals and what stock is held in the store.

Food stuffs are often signed out when used so the Head Chef can see at a glance what stock is used more frequently.

It enables the Chef to see the dates the goods arrived and ensure they are used within the dates on the item.

Old stock is brought forward and used first. New stock is put to the back and used last.

Foods are signed for when delivered and have been checked for dates and damage. This is shown on the stock records.

Damaged stock is not acceptable, this is recorded on the stock sheets so the Chef knows that item is not available.

Only foods that can be made from the stock available will be on the menu.

Stock can be checked regularly and new orders made, this will mean that perishable stock is limited and used as quickly as possible.

Walk in fridges and freezers often have the stock list on the door so you can see at a glance what stock is available.

3 marks for clear, well written and detailed answer that reflects knowledge and understanding of stock control records and their use. The suggestions should be logical and practical.

1–2 marks for answer that covers relevant points with some brief reasons given.

1 mark for outline answer with no explanation. Or answer that is just a list. Or answer that covers only one point but in detail.

5. a) Answer should include:

- Ergonomic features required for a safe and healthy working environment.
- Layout.

- Lighting.
- Heating.
- Services available – gas, electric, water.
- Skill level of chef – what equipment can he use safely.
- Amount of expenditure, costs.
- Type of equipment available.
- Hygiene and Food Safety Act.
- Design and décor.
- Size and extent of menu and market it serves.
- Storage area for food.
- Environmental considerations – how can they reduce, reuse, recycle.

4 marks for clear well written and detailed answer that reflects knowledge and understanding of planning and design of new kitchen area. The suggestions should be logical and practical.

2–3 marks for answer that covers relevant points with some brief reasons given.

1 mark for outline answer with no explanation.

b) Answers should include:

- To check if the new facilities are up to standard.
- Checking on hygiene procedures.
- To look at food storage areas.
- Fridge temperatures.
- Check for pest infestation.
- Check food is fit for sale.
- Check hand washing facilities are available.
- Temperature of cooked foods.
- Correct storage of foods.
- Dates on foods.

4 marks for clear well written and detailed answer that reflects knowledge and understanding of the role of EHO. The suggestions should be logical and practical.

2–3 marks for answer that covers relevant points with some brief reasons given.

1 mark for outline answer with no explanation.

c) Answers should include:

- Give verbal advice on how to keep premises clean and hygienic.

- Advice on the Basic Hygiene Certificate.
- Training sessions for staff.
- Leaflets can be given on safe food practice.
- Advice given on illness and when staff cannot work with food.

1 **mark** for 1 simple answer

2 **marks** for detailed answer with clear explanation

Exam tips

Questions often require specific knowledge and understanding. Candidates may be asked to:

Define: give the meaning of...
List: make a list.
State: write clearly but briefly.
Describe: give an account of...
Discuss: give important aspects of...
           give advantages and disadvantages of ...
Explain: make clear, giving reasons.
Evaluate: give important aspects of...
           give your own opinion of...

Note:
- The questions at the end of the papers will need a high level of understanding and candidates will be expected to discuss, explain or evaluate their answers. These questions are often criteria marked.
- Answering questions in 'bullet points' is popular with candidates *but* often counts as 'writing a list'. Candidates answering questions in this way will not earn good marks for criteria marked questions.

Common errors

Candidates misread questions or see 'key' words and assume they know what the question is about. Examples include:

Fast food – often misinterpreted as 'junk' food, instead of good quality food with fast service.

Food safety – often wrongly considered to be preventing accidents rather than good food hygiene.

Commodities – often wrongly considered to be equipment rather than food.

Tips for candidates

Read each question thoroughly.

Underline key words so you know what the question is asking.

For the essay type questions at the end of the papers, draw up a short plan before starting or highlight key words to help you answer the question.

Look at the number of marks available for the question and write enough to earn the marks.

The exam is not a race – there are no prizes for finishing first.

GOOD LUCK!

Glossary

abdominal pain: pain in the stomach area.

accommodation services: the housekeeping side of an establishment.

accompaniments: items offered separately to main dish.

à la carte: separately priced menu, from which items are prepared and cooked to order

al dente: firm to the bite.

allergic reaction: way in which the body responds to some foods (for example, a rash, swelling or anaphylactic shock).

allergy: an adverse reaction by the body to certain substances (including foods)

attitude: the way in which you approach customers.

appearance: the way you look to customers. It is important to look clean and smart.

au gratin: sprinkled with cheese or breadcrumbs and browned.

bain-marie: container of water to keep foods hot without fear of burning.

BHA: British Hospitality Association.

BII: British Institute of Inn-Keeping.

binary fission: how bacteria multiply by dividing in two.

brûlée: burned cream.

body language: the way in which your body reflects your mood.

bouquet garni: small bundle of herbs.

chefs: staff who are responsible for preparing and cooking food safely and hygienically.

CIEH: Chartered Institute of Environmental Health.

coeliac disease: a serious gluten intolerance. A person with this condition must avoid all forms of wheat, including wholemeal, whole wheat and wheat meal flour, bran, pasta, noodles, semolina, bread, pastry, sauces thickened with flour, muesli, wheat, rye, barley and oat breakfast cereals, beer, and other malted drinks.

complaint: expression of dissatisfaction.

contaminated: containing an additional substance that should not be there.

contract caterers: people who prepare the food for functions such as weddings, banquets, garden parties and parties in private houses. They may prepare and cook the food in advance and deliver it to the venue, or they may cook it on site. They may also provide staff to serve the food if required.

core temperature: temperature in the middle of the food.

corporate: group or chain of businesses. Can be shared, as in uniform or identity.

coulis: sauce made of fruit or vegetable puree.

covers: number of customers.

criteria: the standards and limits judged to be right.

croutons: cubes of bread that are fried or grilled.

customer: a person who buys or uses the products and services.

customer care: how well you look after the paying guests.

décor: how the room is set up and decorated.

diarrhoea: 'the runs'.

EHO: Environmental Health Officer.

en croute: in pastry.

entrée: main course.

evaluation: the assessment of performance.

feedback: information given in response.

fever: a raised temperature.

flambé: cook with flame by burning away the alcohol.

food and drink service: serving area in a restaurant, café or bar.

food hygiene: practices that make sure that food is safe to eat.

food intolerance: condition obliging someone to avoid a certain food because of the effect on their body (e.g. a person with lactose intolerance must avoid milk products).

food poisoning: an illness caught from eating contaminated food.

front-of-house: reception area of an establishment.

garnish: trimming served with the main item.

greeting and seating: how the customers are met and shown to their table.

HACCP: Hazard analysis and critical control points. Stages used in food production to ensure food is safe to eat.

HCIMA: Hotel and Catering International Management Association (now known as the Institute of Hospitality).

High-risk foods: food that provides the perfect conditions for the growth and reproduction of micro-organisms that contaminate the food and make it unsafe to eat.

hospitality and catering industry: businesses that provide food, drink and/or accommodation.

identify: recognise, discover.

industry: business or trade.

in-house: on the premises.

julienne: strips of vegetables cut to matchstick size.

lactose intolerance: condition obliging someone to avoid milk, cheese, butter, yogurt and processed foods that contain milk products.

legislation: laws made and enforced to protect customers.

logo: a printed symbol or trademark used by a company as its emblem.

management: people who are in charge of specific areas.

manner: the way you speak to customers.

marinade: richly spiced liquid used to give flavour and assist in tenderising meat and fish.

mise en place: basic preparation prior to assembling products.

nausea: feeling of sickness.

nutrients: substances found in foods that help us grow and resist infection.

overheads: items a business must pay for before it makes a profit, including materials, workforce, transport and energy.

People 1st: Sector skills council for hospitality, leisure and travel and tourism.

perishable: does not keep well.

personal hygiene: good personal hygiene ensures that germs found in or on the body do not transfer to food.

planning: preparations or arrangements done beforehand.

policies: course of action in place that determines rules (e.g. to enable a safe working environment).

portion control: method used to limit the amount of food a customer is given to the same each time.

promotion: advertising a business to get more trade.

protective: shielding, making safe.

purée: smooth mixture made from food passed through a sieve.

quality: a measure of the level of excellence or standard of a product or service.

quality assurance: a promise or guarantee that services and products are of a particular standard.
quality control: method used to ensure the quality is maintained throughout all stages of making.

reduce: concentrate a liquid by boiling.
regulations: legal requirements.
research: looking at existing products.
response: how you react verbally and in your body language.
review: look back on something and see how it was dealt with.
RIPH: Royal Institute of Public Health.
risk assessment: ways of identifying and preventing accidents.
roux: thickening of cooked flour and fat.
RSPH: Royal Society for the Promotion of Health.

sauce: a liquid that has been thickened.
sauté: tossed in fat.
seating plan: plan of who will be sitting where, on what table.
skill: the ability to carry out something.
SSC: Sector Skills Council.

table d'hôte: menu with fixed courses and limited choice.
time-plan: a logical and ordered plan for a product or event, from start to finish.

wait staff: waiters and waitresses.
wholegrain: using the whole of the grain of wheat.

venue: place where an event is held.
vomiting: being sick.

Index

Note: page numbers in **bold** refer to key word definitions.

Index

Index

Index

operations managers 58
orders, taking 60
organisational skills 67–70
osteoporosis 20, 24
overheads 63–4, 106

packaging
    reduction 126, 127–8
    types 127
    uses 127
panadas 34
paper packaging 127
pasta 30
pastry 35
pastry chefs (patissiers) 4
paysanne cut 32
peas 77, 78–9
pensioners
    afternoon tea for 69
    nutritional needs 104
People 1st 100
personal appearance 90, **91**
personal data, storage of 57
personal hygiene 45–7, 76
phosphorus 24
photographs
    for comparative studies 95, 96
    for event assignments 74
    of work-related experience 84
pigs 28
pizza cafés 69
place cards 67, 69
planning
    comparative studies 97–8, 99
    event assignments 73
    meal 65–7
    practical assessments 75–80
    pub kitchens 143, 149–50
    seating plans 60, **60**
    time plans 67, 76–9
    see also menu planning
plastic 127
poisonous plants 42
polystyrene 127
pork 28, 113
porters 4
    house/linen 58
    kitchen 4
    night 4
portions
    control 64–6, 73, 106, 107
    cost per 81
    size 76
potatoes, creamed 77, 78–9
poultry 28–9
practical assessments 75–81
    choosing dishes 75–6
    costings 75, 81
    equipment lists 79–80
    evaluation 80–1

planning 75–80
    shopping lists 79
preparation skills see food preparation skills
presentation
    of comparative studies 96, 99
    of event assignments 74
    of food 27–8, 40–1, 67–8, 76, 110
    of menus 13
pricing food 81, 106–7
private clients 2
problem-solving 11–13
    complaints procedures 12
    immediate solutions 11
    long-term solutions 11
    and rules and regulations 12
    set procedures for 12
product quality 115
product-and-service providers 1
professional organisations 100–1
profit 106
promotion and sales 67–8, 82–3, 95
protective 86, **86**
protein 20, 22, 103, 104
    and food poisoning 42
    of high biological value (HBV) 22
    of low biological value (LBV) 22
    vegetable 34
purchasing food 54
    see also shopping lists
purée 39

quality assurance/control 13, 115–21
    accommodation ratings 118–21
    judging quality 115–17
questionnaires 68, 95, 96
questions 13
quorn 34

'rare' foods 28–9
Rastafarians 113
receiving food 54
reception areas
    hotels 122–3
    standards of service 88
    see also front-of-house
receptionists 86, 122
    assistant 4
    head 4
    record keeping duties 148
recipes
    choice 75–6
    trials 67, 73
record keeping 7, 132
    for hotels 143, 148
recycling 126, 128
red blood cells 24
reducing 39
regulations 45–6, **46**
reheating 55
reliability 115

Index